60 0083431 4

KT-389-965

Students and External Readers	Staff & Research Students
DATE DUE FOR RETURN	DATE OF ISSUE
-8. OCT. 1973	11 MAR 75 0 0 0 3
1. JUL 74 0 1	12 MAR 76 0 0 5
12 MAR 76 0 0 5	

RESTORATION PURITANISM

RESTORATION PURITANISM

A STUDY OF THE GROWTH

OF ENGLISH LIBERTY

By

Harry Grant Plum

UNIVERSITY LIBRARY NOTTINGHAM

WITHDRAWN

KENNIKAT PRESS
Port Washington, N. Y./London

RESTORATION PURITANISM

Copyright, 1943, by The University of North Carolina Press
Reissued in 1972 by Kennikat Press by arrangement
Library of Congress Catalog Card No: 72-159101
ISBN 0-8046-1644-2

Manufactured by Taylor Publishing Company   Dallas, Texas

FOREWORD

THE STUDENT of English history must long have been dissatisfied with historians' treatment of Restoration Puritanism. This treatment has been due in part to both the classical historians' brilliant but somewhat misleading discussion and our more modern theory of the economic interpretation of history. Professor Green, writing of the Restoration under Charles II, after summing up the work of the Commonwealth, dismissed Puritanism with the single sentence: "All that was noblest and best in Puritanism was whirled away with its pettiness and tyranny in the current of the nation's hate." Macaulay, in his *History of England*, put especial emphasis upon the foibles and extreme views of the radical element, which for Puritanism as a whole is unwarranted and unhistorical. The modern historian, on the other hand, has quite generally ignored the religious problem after 1660 and has emphasized rather the economic, commercial, and constitutional developments, which, after all, must share with religion in the important changes that were shaping the destinies of the English people.

To be sure, the seventeenth century displayed its full portion of prejudice and stubborn conservatism, and in no field have men more readily displaced reason than in the field of religious thought. Few of the pamphleteers of the period displayed any reasonableness, while those who did try to use reason were largely lost in the mass of hostile and vituperative writing. For the modern student it is difficult

[v]

to realize the strong influence which religion exerted upon the man and woman of the seventeenth century. For them as a whole religion was the cement with which society was held together. Nearly all the wars of the century were religious wars. The sanity and logic of later times were sadly lacking, and the Restoration period was one of continuous religious persecution and strife. It is possible that such periods are necessary to purge society of accumulated dross and to strengthen a becoming humility. At least this period of English history accomplished that and at the same time broadened and softened the spirit of both groups of contenders while it aided in placing religion in its proper position as a factor in the development of the individual and the nation.

The seventeenth century was in one sense a very modern century. The earlier discoveries and the conflict with Spain had given birth to a strong national feeling. As a result of the economic revolution, a middle-class society was in the making. Yet these changes, great as they were, had not transformed the thinking of the mass of people to the extent that we sometimes make ourselves believe. The migrations of religious dissenters to the Continent and to the almost unknown new world, even among the intelligent and well-to-do classes, testify to the dominant influence of religion.

If there is any value in these observations, they would seem to warrant an attempt to reëvaluate the events of the Restoration period when there was fought to a successful finish the claim of the Puritan to religious liberty, a claim which was proved to be impossible of divorcement from the larger issue of the liberty of the individual in his relation to both church and state—an issue for which the liberty-loving peoples of the world at this moment, as in the English seventeenth century, are prepared to suffer persecution and death to maintain. It was important for the present-day world that the Anglo-Saxon people settled this problem for themselves so early in their history.

For assistance in collecting the material for this study I must acknowledge the grant of the Social Science Research Council which enabled me to spend a time in the British Museum and the Public Record Office. The coming of the war made it necessary to continue the study in this country, and here I owe especial acknowledgment to the kindness and help of the librarians in the Union Theological Library in New York and in the fine library of Yale University. I must also acknowledge the kindness of Professors Hardin Craig, Wallace Notestein, and C. W. de Kiewiet, who have read the entire manuscript and have given me valuable suggestions, and that of my own colleague, Professor Goldwin Smith, from whose valuable criticisms I have profited. Lastly, my wife's aid and criticism throughout the progress of the work have been of the greatest help.

Most of the general conclusions reached have been the result of a long period of teaching and research in the Stuart period, during which the need of reëvaluating the century in its relation to the modern development of England has taken shape in my mind.

H. G. PLUM

Iowa City, Iowa
July, 1943

CONTENTS

RESTORATION PURITANISM

I

THE BACKGROUND OF

THE RESTORATION

ONE WHO proposes to write of the religion of the sixteenth and seventeenth centuries should first make clear to his readers the meaning which he gives to the term Puritanism. It would be of great service to the general reader if scholars could find a definition to which all would adhere. Such a definition would clarify the term and the history of the period to the general student and often, possibly, to the specialist himself. The century produced many religious groups to which were attached special distinguishing names, and it would seem unnecessary to add to any particular one the additional term of Puritan.

There is needed, now that so many splendid specialized studies have been made of the period and the thought of the time,[1] a new and more general survey that will relate all the characteristic movements of the century and bring this Puritan idea into harmony with them all. No revolutionary period is ever able to break wholly with the past, and these two centuries were peculiarly revolutionary in character. The governmental structure was in process of

1. See especially A. S. P. Woodhouse, *Puritanism and Liberty*; W. K. Jordan, *The Development of Religious Toleration in England*; A. R. Ladell, *Richard Baxter*; T. Lyon, *Religious Liberty in England*; E. D. Bebb, *Nonconformity and Social and Economic Life, 1660-1800*; C. E. Whiting, *Studies in English Puritanism*, and others. For the misuse of the term Puritanism, see Lyon, *op. cit.*, p. 72.

change. The economic life was in process of producing a new society in which feudal relations were to disappear, a free society was to evolve, a middle class was to become articulate, commerce and trade were to become important, and industry was to be developed upon which the commerce was to be based. There was arising a new and fascinating intellectual life which in turn was to become the path by which the English Reformation was to find itself.

Yet all these wonderful new changes were to grow out of and supplement English life and society as it had evolved in the course of centuries. English customs and English common law still persisted. All these new changes must fit themselves into this solid background before they could even begin to add to or supplement ancient law and customs.

In the matter of religion this attachment to the past was especially strong. Through the Middle Ages the church was the strongest, most edifying, and perhaps the best cement of society. It stood for order in a feudal society that tended always toward anarchy. It protected the serf when there was no other protection to be had. It related the hard life of feudal society to a future world in which serfdom would disappear. If the church was universal, the English serf, and even the noble, associated it with English life, his parish, and his English priest. This attitude was always strong even in the clergy themselves so that the transition to a national church was easily made. It changed neither the parish church nor its service, and the higher churchmen fitted into the new structure by their landed relations as well as by their recognition of the authority of the state instead of the Pope of Rome.

The Renaissance in England followed a course of its own. It was critical but it did not, as in the Romance countries of Europe, divorce itself from morals, and it did retain a strong religious spirit. It found many practices to criticize in the Roman church, and its criticism opened the path toward reformation. Thus the Reformation was begun as an effort to reform the church as it had been established by the Roman authority. The Renaissance produced new studies of the Bible, and in the Reformation the Bible became the authority for criticism of all the faults attributed to the old church and the hope of all the changes desired in the new. Through the last half of the sixteenth century, England was torn with religious contention. As the Anglican church developed its peculiar position, its leaders evolved the term of opprobrium which they applied to those who differed with them. The Puritan was the church member who refused to accept the organization based upon the studies and plan of the church as modified and clarified by its so-called father, Richard Hooker, in the *Ecclesiastical Polity.* Those who differed from this program often differed likewise from each other, and while in the main during the sixteenth century they retained their place within the church, it was already clear that such a situation could not continue without disrupting the Anglican structure. The church was Calvinistic with, to be sure, a modified Calvinism in its doctrine. The Puritan had small quarrel with this, but Cranmer had used as the basis for compiling the Book of Common Prayer a number of Catholic service books. The Puritan wished to rid the Anglican church of all these vestiges of the Roman church. Had he wished nothing more, however, Puritanism would fail to hold the attention of students today.

As was said above, at the end of the sixteenth century the body of Puritans remained within the church. England had been but little troubled by heresy as such, and Mary's burnings had created a horror which no statesman or churchman of later times cared to arouse. The church was quite satisfied to allow the King to use the authority of the state to enforce his authority as head of the church, and thus in the early seventeenth century James decreed that the Puritans must conform or be driven out, "harried" from the kingdom. It

was at this point that Puritanism laid claim to the individual
liberty of the subject as founded upon the common law. To
be sure this had never before been applied to the field of
religion, but the Renaissance teachings and the Reformation
itself had made clear the implications of such a claim. Puritanism, at the moment when the Anglican church took definite
action against it, became peculiarly the exponent of individual
liberty in religion as well as of the desire to purify the
English church from all the forms and ornaments of the
old Catholic organization.

When James I issued his fiat in 1604, a considerable number of churchmen left their pulpits. Apparently James had
no notion that action would be needed in respect to the laity
but supposed that when the churchmen were out the laity
would fall into line and a unified church would thus be
established. Perhaps this might have been accomplished if
the cleavage had been clean and those departing from their
pulpits had been prevented from establishing independent
organizations. However, in any case the action could not
have been decisive. The majority of Puritans did not leave
their pulpits. They were the more moderate and more
compromising group who as far as was necessary conformed
but emphasized their individual right to attempt to reform
the practices of the church from within. After 1604 there
was always a Puritan group within the Anglican church who
hoped to modify the prayer book and to broaden the church
teachings.

Puritanism was really the attempt to seize and apply the
spiritual elements of the Reformation movement, to eradi-
cate Roman forms, and to organize the English church so
as to make possible the fullest use by the individual, laity
or clergy, of his historic liberty as established under the law.[2]
From this viewpoint it is confined to no one sect nor is it
excluded from the Anglican church. If Puritanism has any

2. Ladell, *op. cit.*, p. 9.

meaning in the evolution of the nation's history, that meaning results from the solid character, the persistence and action of the moderate element in church and sect. Its real significance arises not in the establishment of any sect, but in the repudiation of the great Roman tradition that papal authority may override individual thought and become the *sine qua non* of man's relationship to his Maker.

It was inevitable from such a background that toleration should make slow progress. It was but partially in harmony with the earlier history of England. There had always been one authoritative church in England, and to the general mind, unity of religion was as important as unity in secular life. The crisis of religion and Puritanism, like that of constitutional liberty, was precipitated by the Stuart attempt at establishing an authoritative government which ignored the nation's historical past. Economic interests might attract the energies of a few, but the nation as a whole regarded their religion as the pivot about which all life and all action turned. The Independents and the Baptists were few in number and were regarded as outside the pale. Elizabeth had driven the small Independent group to Holland, and only after 1604, when James excluded the Presbyterians from the church fold, did the more radical separatist groups begin to thrive.

It is true that at this point, 1604, the problem became difficult. The nation was Christian, and the excluded groups had apparently lost their citizenship in so far as they refused to conform. That comparatively few members left the church in 1604 is explained in part by the fact that in the seventeenth century few persons believed that church and state could be separated or the church be other than a unit. How could the church comprehend the nation and still allow liberty of the individual conscience? A broader basis for the church must be found, and Presbyterian especially, but in the main Independent too, believed that such a basis

could be found and that all could be comprehended within
the church with enough liberty to satisfy the individual conscience. Certainly the main body of Puritans remained
within the church and were found there when the Long
Parliament broke with the King in 1642. The Puritans who
had fled to New England under the Laudian regime included
many of the radical group and also came largely from within
the church.[3] Mildly Presbyterian-Puritan, they saw Laud's
policy as destroying their liberty and fled to a new country
to set up their own religious organization.

There is another aspect of the Puritan period that has emphasized the idea that the Puritan was to be entirely excluded from the church after the settlement of James I. The
parliaments of the Stuart period were continually hostile to
the Stuart theory of government. They were strongly Puritan, as was the nation, and believed that the Stuart dynasty
was radically opposed to that which as Englishmen they had
cherished. The more they became aware of the past, the
stronger grew their opposition to the King's program. They,
too, were conscious of the long fight for the freedom of the
individual against Noble and King. They had secured the
great charter of liberties, the courts, and the common law.
As the period of Wentworth and Laud was reached they saw
the character of the struggle more clearly. Puritan and Parliament joined forces for the struggle to bind the hands of
King and churchmen for the purpose of securing liberty in
constitutional, civil, and religious matters. Moreover, as has
been suggested, the main bodies of the parliaments during
this period were Puritan in the religious sense, as was proved
when the Long Parliament determined to oppose the King
with arms. Even of those who left the Parliament at this
juncture and went with the King, there were some who, like
Lucius Carey, had no heart in his cause, but were afraid of
the consequences of rebellion.

3. Woodhouse, *op. cit.*, pp. 55-57. Mr. Woodhouse does not include in
his definition of Puritan the liberal group within the Anglican church.

The Revolution of 1640-1648 was Puritan because this opposition to the King had first developed about the religious problem, but its success in its early and constructive stage, the legislation signed by Charles I, was due to the strong support of the conforming Puritan, who had become convinced that the liberty of Englishmen was at stake. The weakness of the Parliament in the struggle with Charles I lay primarily in the religious field. Parliament had never secured the initiative in religious matters. Under the Tudor rulers it had merely confirmed action taken by the Crown. To this constitutional weakness were added now the religious differences emphasized by the action of James in 1604. Under Charles, the work of Archbishop Laud seemed, to all moderate churchmen and to the Puritan laity, to be destroying the historical church. The Puritan Parliament was strongly opposed to Laud's work primarily, but also to the strengthening of Charles's arbitrary power which in fields other than religious was clearly destroying the historical rights of Parliament and encroaching upon individual liberty.

The bitter controversies of the Long Parliament brought forward the most uncompromising Puritan leaders, Presbyterianism of the Scottish type rather than English Puritan Presbyterianism. Under such circumstances a settlement of the religious problem by the Long Parliament was exceedingly difficult. Had Pym lived, even he probably would have failed to find a satisfactory compromise; but his early death made any such effort futile, and civil war was the inevitable result. It is the religious side of the controversies in this period that has led historians rightly to characterize this as the Puritan revolution, but it should be recalled that it had fundamentally in mind the individual liberty of Englishmen threatened by a despotic king.

It was no easy matter to shape one's course at such a time and in such a struggle. As remarked above, the seventeenth century was distinctly religious in the sense that all else flowed from religion.[4] Especially with the conforming Puritan, it meant loyalty to principle and institutions as against loyalty to person, and when Charles set up his standard in Oxford the hard choice must be made. Little wonder that Falkland as well as many another found the decision hardly possible, but their difficulty helps to explain why Puritanism has been so long considered as a religious movement rather than as a principle of individual liberty.

In this sense then, Puritanism links itself with liberalism in the attempt to recognize and keep step with the changes made necessary by the growth of a complex society without the loss of all that society has accomplished, a salvaging of what is useful for the future. Puritanism was not revolutionary but rather evolutionary in its purpose. To guard the individual, to secure for him liberty of thought and action in religion so far as it was compatible with the ends of society, was its consistent end and aim. To restrict the powers of an arbitrary government; to free the individual from the authority of an arbitrary church whether guided by religious or secular authority; to reinterpret the common law to establish a society of free individuals; and to reshape society to fit the needs of free men in all the aspects of the social need: these constituted the ideals and purposes of Puritanism. That we have tended to apply the term to the religious problem alone does not change its meaning or purpose. The complexity of every phase of the movement very naturally brought out a variety of opinion as diverse as human thought and human needs. In forms of government, in religious organization, in economic affairs were to be found the conservative, the liberal, and the radical, each with the ramifications of thought that for the time seemed to produce chaos and to destroy all social continuity. It is both interesting and

4. See Hugh Peters in Whitehall debates (Woodhouse, *op. cit.*, pp. 137-39). It is interesting to note that in his objections to the overthrow of the church in the French Revolution Burke places religion as the foundation of society and the moral basis of the state.

important that in the field of religion the Puritan tended, in the great majority of cases, to the liberal rather than the radical viewpoint.

The coming of the war on the removal of Charles from London tended to emphasize the idea of the willing separation of the Nonconformists from the Anglican church instead of the almost general acceptance by the Puritan of the need of such a state organization.[5] Both the Presbyterian and Independent Puritans strongly favored a state church until the protest of the bishops made it clear that the Anglican organization was opposed to any compromise. First the Independent then the Presbyterian came to believe that the church, like the King, must be conquered by force of arms and the church remodeled in a more liberal spirit.

The appeal of Parliament to the Scots for military aid gave the Presbyterians their chance. They were a majority in Parliament, but they were in disagreement about accepting the Covenant and the organized Scottish church as a basis of the English organization. Baillie, the Scottish commissioner, reported this hesitancy and saw in the Parliament's modification of the commission's agreement an intent to evade the issue. There was little sympathy, especially among the English laity, for the Scottish church, and when the agreement was put into effect, few districts made the changes necessary for the Presbyterian establishment, since the terms left a freedom of interpretation.[6] Unfortunately, the trials of civil war emphasized and strengthened the radical element. Power passed from Parliament to the army. Pride's purge eliminated the Presbyterian group, which clung to the support of Charles as King, and in the end the radicals murdered the King and took control of the government.

This brief survey of the civil war period has been made to place in as clear perspective as possible the reasons for the

5. See Lyon, *op. cit.*, pp. 77 ff.

6. Woodhouse, *op. cit.*, Introduction; Ladell, *op. cit.*, pp. 26, 28. Baxter testified to the English lay opposition to the Scottish church.

failure of the movement to secure any satisfactory solution for either the religious or the constitutional problems. Until the capture of the King, the serious nature of the military problem had checked differences of opinion. Perhaps, too, the country was largely ignorant of the development of radicalism in the army. When, however, the destruction of the King's forces and his capture gave a breathing space, there was seen to have developed in the army a radicalism in which the Parliamentary party could have no part. Could they have had any trust in the King's word, or had he been killed in battle, the problem might have been solved by the acceptance of his young son as King, bound by the legislation which his father had signed before the essay to arms had begun. The majority of the Parliament had no wish to destroy the King, but they were unable to find any satisfactory way to control him. Their long discussion gave the military their chance. The purging of the Presbyterian members left the small "rump" ready to accept the army's dictates. The King was murdered and the country as a whole estranged.

The small Parliament left after the purge and the death of the King had no chance. The army quickly repudiated them and a military dictatorship came into being with Cromwell, a fortunate choice, as dictator, though never free from army control. Thus Cromwell began his rule with the nation's opposition. His wars in Scotland and Ireland conciliated many, his foreign policy conciliated the trading classes, his religious policy gave him the adherence of the Presbyterians. The people as a whole accepted his efforts to unite Scotland and Ireland with England. They had no criticism for the position in which he placed the nation abroad. The progress of the general welfare they accepted but gave praise with reluctance. His outraging of the spirit of the constitution they could not forgive. The historic principle of government by King, Lords and Commons they dared not disclaim.

When the Commonwealth took over the government, the great majority of the clergy remained in office. If we look forward to the return of Charles II, it will be found that but about 2,500 of the 9,500 parishes were vacated. It is probable that many of the clergy were sympathetic with Nonconformity, many no doubt being Puritan enough to keep a clear conscience. There were some, we know, who felt that they could best support their own cause by keeping office, holding communion, quietly or in secret,[7] using the prayer book by committing its prayers to memory, and acquiescing in the liberty granted by Cromwell's government. No question was raised concerning either Presbyterian or Baptist. Both were needed, and the laws prohibited only Roman and Anglican, while after 1653 Cromwell tended strongly toward a liberal state church with full toleration for all those beyond its pale. He was criticized for his liberalism by Presbyterian and Independent; yet Presbyterians worked consistently and harmoniously with the government. Their dissatisfaction was due largely to the fear that toleration would weaken the government, encourage rebellion, and strengthen Catholicism.[8]

The period was long enough to give emphasis to the spiritual side of the Puritan ideal. Cromwell's legislation, aimed at the reformation of manners, bore some fruit in spite of the prevalence of coarseness and brutality. He relied for its accomplishment rather upon education and religion than upon legislation. The opposition of the Puritan to the Book of Sports of James I had been based on the belief that it struck at the moral basis of religion upon which the state

7. Evelyn makes frequent reference to the practice. See Woodhouse, *op. cit.*, Introduction, and Jordan, *op. cit.*, III, 195, note, and 201.

8. Both Baxter and Calamy thought Cromwell too liberal because of the known intrigues of both Anglican and Roman as well as the political extremists.

must needs rely. Charles II found that even the Anglican had become convinced of this and reasserted the Puritan Sabbath law early in his reign while issuing declarations against profanity and other evils.

The revenue from confiscated church lands was used to a large extent in the interest of education. Cromwell, himself more interested in higher education, commended the work of Oxford and Cambridge and founded a new university in Durham from the revenues of that wealthy and extensive bishopric. He urged the scholars to piety as being as important as learning, and when he found them zealous for education left many of the Anglicans in their professorships. He was induced to set up a commission in London to certify teaching candidates but allowed it no doctrinal tests. Many schools for the poor as well as for the middle class were set up. The large parishes were divided, the smaller ones united, and better provision was made for the ministers.

A beginning was made toward seeing religion as a social force. Puritanism was learning to care for its own poor. Hospitals for the care of the sick were founded. If religion was the guiding force, it was to be determined by one's life rather than by profession. If life was a preparation for a future world, it was to be judged by its fruit, and at least for the time being, man, not God, was to be the judge. Cromwell was the first English ruler whose "political ideals were the direct outcome of his creed."[9]

Puritanism in these few years had given something to England that was to remain. In his *Areopagitica* Milton had set forth the first great classical defense of liberty—a noble defense set on broad bases, with clear definitions, argued with fervor yet with a clear, cold logic that could not be denied. It set the rights of the individual over against the powers of the state and the organized church and might

9. S. R. Gardiner, *Cromwell's Place in History*, p. 426; Jordan, *op. cit.*, III, 194 ff.

well have been a guide to Locke's later theories of government and religious toleration. It put emphasis upon a free
press and liberty of conscience, and upon the law as the basis
of these rights. It could have been a profitable textbook for
English sovereigns for a hundred years. On its practical side,
too, Puritanism had been constructive. Pepys and Evelyn,
the latter always bitter toward Cromwell, witnessed to the
kindly character, the leniency, the firmness, and the advances
of the Puritan effort. 'Clergy and people gained a confidence
that sustained the Nonconformist through the thirty years of
bitter persecution which were to follow. When the end came,
"the dullest understood that a great thing had gone from the
world."[10] It is irrational to think that all this positive effort
was to be forgotten and lost to the nation.'

But the revolution was nearing its close. During the Civil
War period, London had largely financed the Parliamentary
forces.[11] In spite of Cromwell's successes abroad and their
effect on commerce, the city grew tired of the military power
and longed for a settled government. The death of Oliver
precipitated a crisis. Presbyterian influence in the city had
grown, and it strongly favored the return of Charles II
and the reëstablishment of the dynasty and the two houses of
Parliament. The army leaders were jealous of each other.
Fleetwood acknowledged Richard and commanded the city.
Lambert, after his quick success against a rising in the West,
moved his forces northward to sound out Monck's views and
get control of his forces. The armies too were tired of war.
Monck, waiting long enough, found the disintegration of
Lambert's forces complete and, imprisoning the leader, he
marched to London proclaiming himself prepared to sub-
ordinate the army to the civil power when that power should
be established. He quickly forced himself into control of
affairs, made his peace with the city, saw to it that the Long

10. J. Buchan, *Oliver Cromwell*, p. 444.
11. M. Wren, London in the Puritan Revolution.

Parliament was recalled; and when provision was made for
a Convention Parliament to settle the affairs of the king
dom, saw it adjourn and peacefully depart into oblivion.[12]

The rest of the way was easy. With the Declaration of
Breda Charles had announced his intention to respect "liberty
of tender consciences" and the "rights of Parliament." So
on the invitation of the Convention Parliament, Charles came
home amid the rejoicings of his people. The nation had never
accepted the Puritan revolution and for the moment forgot
what it had produced. Yet behind the consciousness of the
moment, when the old settled order had been restored and
the course of events began to appear, there came back slowly
and more fully than ever before the issue of liberty in religion
and government, of morality and piety in contrast to the in-
decencies, coarseness, and immorality of the court and society;
and when the issue was put squarely up to the nation, there
was no hesitation. The Revolution of 1688 was quietly
effected in government and religion.

12. George Monck, *A Collection of Several Letters and Declarations.*
I have not followed Monck's intentions through the period. It is enough
for my purpose to note that he was satisfied with the final results.

II

THE RESTORATION

THE CONVENTION Parliament which recalled Charles II was predominantly Presbyterian.[1] The members might fail to pass legislation without some help from the Independents but certainly no legislation could pass without their approval. They with the Independents elected the speaker, and Reynolds, Calamy, Manton and Baxter, all Presbyterians, preached and prayed for the House.[2] As soon as the call had been sent to the King, the House set to work to put things in order. A committee was appointed to bring in a bill to establish the church on the basis of Charles's declaration, a bill to settle the property question, known finally as the Act of Indemnity and Oblivion. All the measures went slowly. Petitions crowded in upon the House. There was much disagreement and wrangling over the terms of the bill to settle property. The Anglicans were impatient to secure both their properties and the control of offices. The radical groups were certain only of ill usage and took advantage of conditions to incite riots and make trouble for the govern-

1. Louise Brown, "The Religious Factors in the Convention Parliament," *English Historical Review*, XXII, 51. Miss Brown's study is incomplete in that it fails to make clear the Presbyterian position in favor of comprehension rather than toleration as being the reason for their disagreement with the Independents. See also H. W. Clark, *History of English Nonconformity*, I, 10 ff.

2. *House Journals*, 1660, pp. 1 and 8.

ment. The House of Lords replaced the lower house's resolution on the rights of Parliament by one of their own: "That
according to the fundamental laws of the Kingdom, the
government is and ought to be by King, Lords and Commons."[3] This the House accepted, and Charles had no
objection to the form or matter.[4] He urged haste with the
indemnity and oblivion bill, and this was completed before
the prorogation and signed by the King.

The religious question was more difficult. The House
prepared its bill by July, but the Lords, influenced by the
Anglican bishops, distorted it with amendments to which
for the most part the House refused to agree. When the
first prorogation came, Charles through Clarendon announced
that he would give the Parliament more specific religious instructions and shortly issued them in the form of a moderately
liberal declaration.[5] When Parliament reconvened, a new
bill was drawn in harmony with Charles's declaration, and
upon this the House worked until nearly the close of the
session. In the meantime the supply had been voted and
most matters were in order. Charles, probably because he
was fearful of disagreement or because he was not in sympathy with the bill before the House, announced that he was
soon to appoint a committee to recommend a religious settlement.[6] Perhaps because of this announcement the effort to
agree upon the bill failed, and the matter was left to Charles's
committee.[7]

There has been a general tendency to minimize the part
taken by the Presbyterian Puritans in the Restoration or to
suggest that they were outmanoeuvred and inefficient in the

3. *Ibid.*, pp. 3-7; *Lords Journals*, 1660, p. 8.
4. *House Journals*, 1660, pp. 10-11.
5. *Lords Journals*, 1660, pp. 180-82.
6. One of Miss Brown's arguments for the Presbyterian minority is
based on these votes. It must be recalled that Charles's announcement
preceded these votes and may have determined at least some votes which
ordinarily would have been Presbyterian.
7. Clark, *op. cit.*, II, 12-14; cf. Miss Brown's article, note 6.

part they played. It is worth while to call attention to the
fact that they had ever been monarchical in their attitude, had
faithfully backed the Long Parliament in its efforts to tie
the King's hands by legislative action, and, while supporting the civil war against the King, had strongly advocated
agreement with him until the radical army drove them from
Parliament. In general the Presbyterians had not sympathized with the terms of the Scottish alliance and, when in
1643 the Scottish Covenant was accepted in England, they
were half-hearted in effecting the organization of a Presbyterian church.

The English Presbyterians were distinctly English and
Puritan in their make-up, and to them comprehension meant
only the Anglican acceptance of certain changes in organization and ritual which should give a freedom of individual
action beyond that which Charles I and Laud had contem-
plated.[8] They believed in the state church, but a divinely
ordained state church was to their way of thinking impossible
to accept. Their greatest antipathy was to the Roman church
because of its foreign and arbitrary control over men's lives.
They asked only for Archbishop Usher's plan,[9] which
would have combined the two systems and have given a modified democratic control, leaving room for individual initiative; but they opposed toleration because toleration would
have admitted the Roman group which they feared beyond
the devil himself. Hence they declined to accept the program of the Independents for a general toleration, and, if
they had ever had it, lost the support of Charles II, who
favored toleration in order to give a legal status to Roman
Catholics. From this position they never wavered through
the long period of persecution which followed,[10] although

8. Clark, *op. cit.*, II, 10. Both Baxter and Calamy emphasized this.
The laity were especially hostile to Scotch Presbyterianism. See Ladell,
Richard Baxter, p. 24.
9. Baxter especially emphasized the Presbyterian approval of the Usher
plan.   10. Clark, *op. cit.*, I, 10 ff.

they came to embrace toleration as an alternative when it excluded the Catholics.

On coming to London, Charles at once appointed a group of ten Presbyterians as chaplains and later designated them together with a group of bishops to consider the proposed religious settlement. The latter, however, refused to meet the Presbyterians, and Charles then proposed the conference at Savoy; it was undoubtedly this announcement that influenced the Convention Parliament to put aside the bill for religious settlement[11] to be considered by a new Parliament. Before the dissolution of the Convention Parliament, the attitude of the Anglican bishops and the council had become clear. Speaking to the Lords at the dissolution after the King had retired, Clarendon had thanked God that so many of the displaced bishops had been able to return so that the office of the consecration of priests might be passed on to the new generation of churchmen unimpaired.[12]

Charles II generally lost patience with the slowness of his parliaments, and his message to the Convention Parliament that he was about to appoint a commission for the revision of the prayer book may have been no more than the loss of patience. It certainly influenced the general feeling that Charles was still prepared to stand by his Declaration. Soon after the dissolution, Charles appointed a committee of Presbyterian divines and another of Anglican churchmen headed by Archbishop Juxon, to whom he presented the task, to be accomplished within four months, of settling the government of the church and revising the prayer book. This resulted in the famous Savoy Conference.

There was much uncertainty as to the procedure of the Commission. Satisfied with things as they were, the Anglicans insisted that the Presbyterians present a complete statement of the changes demanded, leaving the Anglicans to

11. *Ibid.*, I, 14; Edmund Calamy, *The Nonconformist's Memorial*, I, 20-22.

12. *Lords Journals*, 1660-1665, p. 239.

review the list and to accept or reject it in part or in whole. When the Presbyterians found that they were to have no chance to debate the matter, they lost heart, and only at the last moment did Baxter somewhat hastily draw up a statement of the desired changes which was accepted by the Presbyterian group, and five members were chosen to present the request to the bishops.[13]

At this session the Presbyterians found themselves overwhelmed and embarrassed, and only Baxter and Calamy attempted to defend their position. The discussion was very brief, and the bishops agreed to prepare and send their answer to the Presbyterian group in due time. When the answer was finally sent it was found to be a complete denial of the changes asked for. The Presbyterians then drew up a general defense of their position[14] which was later supplemented by *The Humble and Earnest Petition of Others in the Same Commission*. This procedure, which had dragged over the period allotted for the revision, ended the work of the conference. It was clear that few among the Anglicans were prepared to make any compromise that would admit the Presbyterian clergy to a place within the Anglican fold. It was in fact stated by Archbishop Juxon that, had it been thought that the position taken by the Anglican clergy would have won over any Presbyterian, the conditions would have been made more uncompromising.

The issues were later debated in many pamphlets. Altogether the Presbyterians seem to have had the better of the argument in the presentation of the respective positions. Their pamphlets are characterized by more sober thought and reasoned argument[15] and by a broader grasp of the problems

13. *The Grand Debate between the most Reverend Bishops and the Presbyterian Divines appointed by his Sacred Majesty as Commissioners for the Review and Alteration of the Book of Common Prayer.*

14. Richard Baxter, *A Petition for Peace with Reformation of the Liturgy as it was presented to the Right Reverend Bishops by the Divines.*

15. *Ibid.*; Edmund Calamy and Others, *An Exact Collection of Farewell Sermons Preached by the Late London Ministers.*

at stake; they were able to point to Anglican writers who
supported their views, to Jeremy Taylor, Edward Stillingfleet,[16] Archbishop Usher and others. Anglican pamphlets,
on the other hand, were naturally filled with the bitterness
of long-suppressed desires and hopes and the antagonism and
enmity of a group driven from office and in many cases from
the country. How much influence the pamphlets may have
had it is difficult to say, but they at least make clear to the
present-day reader the great significance of the issue at stake
—a free conscience, individual self-respect, and liberty of
thought.

With the efforts of the Commission out of the way, the
Convocation appointed a committee of twenty members with
eighty-five clerks to review and revise the liturgy and prayer
book. Some few of the Presbyterian suggestions were introduced, very cursory and superficial revisions were made,
and the report was accepted by the Convocation and presented to Parliament for its sanction. But even the Cavalier
Parliament put little faith in the sincerity of the revision
and, after some delay and debate, finally accepted it by a
vote of ninety-six to ninety votes. The debate raised the
question of the right of the Convocation to proceed independently of Parliament and indicated as well dissatisfaction
with the work done.[17]

The failure of the Savoy Conference had a far-reaching
effect. A considerable number of the Presbyterians remained
in office even though they disliked the new liturgy. They
felt it wise to remain in order to try for further reform and
reopen the way for the inclusion of their brethren. The
general body of Presbyterian pastors refused to accept a
prayer book made public only on the day on which their
acceptance or rejection was to be announced, and left the

16. Stillingfleet's *Irenicum: A Weapon Salve for the Church's Wounds*
gave offense to the Anglican church on account of its liberalism.

17. Norman Sykes, *Church and State in England in the Eighteenth
Century*, pp. 11 ff.

Anglican church.[18]   There was thus established a strong body of dissent which was to make most difficult a final settlement of the religious problem and which was to trouble the church through the rest of the Stuart period.   For the great problem of the seventeenth century, the problem of individual liberty, the exclusion was of great significance. It made it clear to the largest and strongest body of Nonconformists that since the church would have none of them, their only course must be to throw in their lot with the other sects, and gradually in the twenty years following, the Presbyterian leaders came out on the side of and in full support of toleration. So again under the later Stuarts, the leadership of the opposition to absolute government in church or state is found in the religious group which from the Tudor period had stood for individual liberty as against the absolutist idea of authority.[19]

Charles's first regular parliament, the Cavalier Parliament, met in May, 1661.   The King in his address to them emphasized the need of religious peace: "The peace of State is concerned in peace of Religion.   There is no order in civil affairs when there is none in ecclesiastical affairs."   The address commended the Presbyterians for their moderation, their attachment to the episcopal form of government, their learning and piety.   The King declared against the use of the prayer book until the ecclesiastical problem should be settled.   Clarendon, who addressed Parliament after the King had retired, gave quite a different color to the problem and made quite clear what the Anglicans desired from Parliament.[20]   The House began to work without delay.   A general committee was at once appointed for religion.   By the time the Convocation's recommendations regarding the

18. *Ibid.*, pp. 12 ff.   It was probably off the press some two weeks but had not yet become available.

19. Sykes contends that the organization of the party opposition to Charles II in 1672 was due to this group.

20. *Lords Journals*, 1661, p. 179.

Book of Common Prayer were disposed of, the bill for the government of corporations was ready for introduction. While this was going through its regular course, the bill which became the Act of Uniformity was introduced and had some discussion in the House before the prorogation, at which time the King gave his sanction to the Corporation Act in December 1661. Early in 1662 the Act of Uniformity was agreed to by both houses of Parliament, and Charles gave it his assent. This was followed in 1663 by the Conventicle Act. Later, after the cessation of the plague in 1665, the Five Mile Act was passed.

These four acts constituted the famous Clarendon Code and set definitely the policy of the Restoration toward religion. They provided for the exclusion of all Nonconformists in borough and local government, made obligatory the repudiation of the Covenant, exacted an oath to support the King and to abhor all opposition to his authority, and to accept and use the Book of Common Prayer as the one church service. All services outside the parish church were made illegal, and a fine and imprisonment were fixed as punishment for such illegal preaching. Finally the Five Mile Act forbade any Nonconformist pastor to reside within five miles of any borough where he had formerly preached to or had charge of a congregation.

The first act was intended to destroy the political influence of the Presbyterians and other sects, while the second was intended to eliminate the Presbyterians or drive them into dissent. The Act of Uniformity made impossible the exercise of any religious or educational work within the established church unless the minister was prepared to abjure the Covenant, use the Book of Common Prayer, and take an oath to support the King, whatever he might choose to do. The Presbyterian clergy and those of other sects gave up their pulpits. As nearly as it is possible to estimate the numbers, about two thousand Presbyterians and five hundred Inde-

pendents were forced out of the church at this time.[21] Most
of them did not wait for the act to come into legal effect.
A considerable number, when they read the act, decided to
remain within the Anglican church, but it is impossible to
say how many.[22] The London ministers addressed a protest to Charles and received Charles's assurance that the law
would be modified by an indulgence, but by this time few
put much trust in Charles's word. In 1662 a volume of farewell sermons preached in the city of London was issued.[23]
In it very generally the advice is given to attend the Anglican services, to be constant in godly service, and to take
punishment meekly; and the hope is expressed of a return
at some future time. This readiness to accept a situation
and act according to law should perhaps have been taken by
the Anglican church as evidence of the character and godli-
ness of the displaced ministry, but there is nothing in any of
the writings to suggest that it was. The church was jubilant
at its easy success and determined to destroy Nonconformity.

It should be recognized that the government had reason
during the early period of the Restoration for severe measures against Nonconformity. The more radical sects had
not waited for Charles's return to show their opposition to
the Restoration movement. The Fifth Monarchy Men,
together with many of Cromwell's old soldiers, saw in the

21. Calamy, *Nonconformist's Memorial*; G. Lyon Turner, *Original
Records of Early Nonconformity*, III, 35-65.

22. Robert Halley in his *Lancashire, its Puritanism and Nonconformity*
finds three out of one hundred remaining. Reynolds and one or two more
accepted bishoprics. No attempt to establish the number has been found
by the author. Lancashire had been a stronghold of Presbyterians who
were so confident of Breda that almost a solid delegation of Cavaliers was
sent to the first Parliament of the Restoration. In 1689 the city of
Lancaster was emphatically Jacobean (see p. 344).

23. Calamy and others, *An Exact Collection of Farewell Sermons*. It
contained sermons by Calamy, Watson, Jacomb, Case, Sclater, Baxter,
Jenkin, Manton, Lye, and Collins. In a subsequent edition there were
added sermons by Bates, Brook, Mede, Caryl, Seeman, Venin, Newcomen,
Cradicot, Bull, Pledger, and Bierman. Baxter had left his congregation
in Kidderminster earlier and had come up to London.

Restoration the destruction of their hopes, and for some
time after the government was settled, small rebellions and
riots continued to occur. Parliament was no doubt influenced
by these disorders in shaping the laws, but it is significant that
from the beginning the churchmen took the initiative in
shaping the Clarendon Code and were active in the execution
of the acts long after there could be any fear of revolt.

To supply twenty-five hundred new places within the
church was no easy matter, and all too many unfit ministers
were set over the churches. The discontent which this soon
caused and the pleas of the congregations to their old ministers led to a changed Nonconformist policy before the end
of the year 1662. By that time both Presbyterian and Con-
gregationalist had decided that since the Act of Uniformity
did not forbid preaching outside the parish church, the work
might go on as supplementing the inefficient work of the Anglican ministry. This new policy was met in 1663 by the
Conventicle Act,[24] which refused the right of the dissenters
to preach or teach anywhere to more than five persons in
addition to the family. The new act was not received in the
spirit of resignation that yielded to the earlier act. By this
legislation the government had made itself as responsible as
the Anglican group to enforce the law. There followed a
period of earnest and passionate persecution. Officials were
everywhere brought to hand, the churchmen were in accord
and the informers busy. Persecution had, however, all too
little effect. The Anglican church had assumed that, driven
into dissent, the ministers would soon lose their influence and
Anglicanism would stand supreme. This, however, did not
follow. Too many churchmen were averse to active persecution, too many borough officials refused to enforce the law.
The informers were soon repudiated by local officials, and
the King, uneasy perhaps at the inclusion of Catholics and

24. The Statutes at Large, collected by Danby Pickering, VIII, 209;
hereafter referred to as Pickering, Statutes.

at the complaints boldly asserting his forgotten promises, issued in 1662 a Declaration of Indulgence to alleviate persecution. Parliament at its early meeting objected to this and it was withdrawn, but its effect was to emphasize lenity in some quarters and to strengthen resistance in others.

The early period—1662-1665—definitely established the Nonconformist opposition to the efforts of government and church. The government as well as the church early assumed that every small and large movement of dissatisfaction with government policy was directed by the religious opposition. The jails were filled with all sects but especially with Friends and Anabaptists. The church, too, overemphasizing the Nonconformist sympathy with political discontent, ere long had crystallized religious opposition. In 1662 the Presbyterian ministers had advised their congregations to conform to the laws, attend the services, and if dissatisfied, supplement the service with reading sermons and scripture. Complaints against the ignorance and the evil lives of some of the conformist clergy soon changed the character of the advice. Nonconformist pastors and laity went to prison or paid fines, and those in prison were cared for by the faithful. When in 1663 the Code was strengthened by the Conventicle Act, which was intended to separate pastor and people, it was disobeyed or some newly ordained minister took up the work. Many of the churchmen revolted against the persecutions, the borough officials were lax or refused to take the testimony of informers. Many Presbyterians attended church services and partook of communion; hence in many localities they were elected to office in the boroughs, and these refused where possible to prosecute cases. The church was well aware of the unfitness of many churchmen. The Convention Parliament had legalized the return of deprived churchmen but had emphasized the limitation to but one benefice. The ink was hardly dry upon the statute before the church had sanctioned the breaking of it. It was notorious that some bishops had no religious interest in their dioceses. The need of supplying 2,500 places in the church in 1662 had brought in many timeservers. The court of Charles proceeded to set a very poor example in discipline of character. The rabble followed the court practice with enthusiasm, and many churchmen found the moral laxness to their taste.

In 1662-1663, the Archbishop of Canterbury issued a set of "Articles of Visitation" for the use of the dioceses, and his example was followed by most of the bishops. These efforts, however, were ineffectual in the face of opposite example. The careful churchmen were busy hunting out those who neglected to come to church or, coming, refused communion. Many, of course, who were spiritually inclined and who loved the church service, yet had sympathy for those who remained outside, kept their Christian character, and were honest and industrious.[25]

When the plague began in 1665 and grew worse day by day, many of the conformist ministers fled their posts, partly because they were timeservers only and partly because services were largely discontinued and the Anglicans had not yet developed the habit of visiting the homes and carrying on the pastoral work. Many, of course, fled through fear. The Nonconformist clergy very readily stepped into the breach, took up the pastoral work, ministered to the sick, buried the dead, and preached in the vacant pulpits unless the authorities forbade. It was the period when any wavering of the Nonconformist flock had been changed to steadfastness and when generally the tide was turned against persecution. So also the unrest among the soldiers of the Commonwealth, the Fifth Monarchy Men, and Republicans, was largely passing. The fears of the reëstablished monarchy were allayed, and the government had less reason for persecution of religion for political purposes.

25. J. H. Overton, *Life in the English Church, 1660-1714*, pp. 7-15.

Complaints were also rife by 1665 of the economic consequences of the government's religious policy. In one pamphlet it was complained that thirty or forty thousand men
active in trade and commerce had been driven from the country or despoiled and that England was suffering in conse-
quence. With less reason, yet with some, perhaps, the author
complained that funds needed for commerce were being taken
in large amounts to turn into plate for the churches or were
lying idle in the hands of the clergy. The author maintained that £450,000 were being drawn from use each year
by the clergy where £200,000 could easily maintain them.[26]
It was seen very early that the middle classes, especially the
trading classes, were the main supporters either openly or
covertly of the Nonconformist groups, and from 1664 to
1672 the pamphlets discussing the economic results of the
persecutions increased in numbers, emphasis, and definite-
ness.[27]

There seems little doubt that the church suffered greatly
from its activity as police officer for both church and state.[28]
The churchmen assumed the attitude of coercion and gave
more attention relatively to this aspect of their work than to
the regular offices of the church. This, with the loosening
of morals at the court, tended to spread the contagion of immorality throughout England and thus strengthened Nonconformist activity. There was much attention given to the
work of education by the Nonconformist clergy. Many well-
to-do families employed them as tutors and chaplains. Schools
were organized by Nonconformist ministers, sometimes with
the support of individual conformist clergymen, sometimes

26. *Et a Dracone, or some Reflections upon a Letter out of the West
called Omnia, a Bello Comesta.* These two argued the economic effects
of persecution over a period of several years. See also Samuel Fortney,
England's Interest and Improvement; and an anonymous pamphlet, *The
Way to be Rich according to the Practice of the Great Audley.*
    27. The Seligman collection of economic documents in Columbia Uni-
versity contains the most important of these.
    28. *Protestant Dissenters Magazine,* I, 142.

independently of any support other than themselves, and in spite of efforts to destroy them, they continued to thrive.[29]

By late 1665 three years had passed in the effort to destroy Nonconformity. Persecution had been bitter and all the arguments possible had been used to justify it. In spite of its severity it had failed to accomplish its purpose, and many liberal Anglicans had come to doubt its effectiveness. The government, too, felt more secure; the small rebellions or riots had been mostly dispersed. The local officials were less interested in the success of the Anglican church; some were disgusted with the severity of its methods and many were sympathetic with the persecuted. Many well-to-do members of the local community gave them support, thus intimidating the Anglican effort and offering an excuse for the justices to ignore the matter. It seemed a time to take stock, to see how effective the efforts had been.

In 1665 Archbishop Sheldon asked of his bishops a survey of each diocese to discover the number of Nonconformist ministers, their places of residence, and the numbers of the laity.[30] The reports came in slowly; twenty out of twenty-six bishops seem to have ignored the request, or their reports have been completely lost. One, the Bishop of St. Asaph in Wales, simply reported that there were no Nonconformists in the diocese![31] The reports were certainly discouraging to the archbishop, in so far as they came. Whether Nonconformity had grown or diminished—and both contentions were

---

29. See Turner, *op. cit.*, II, for lists of well-to-do supporters; Baxter, *The Poor Husbandman's Advocate*, pp. 1-25. In his memorial to Thomas Goudge (p. 23), Baxter states that Goudge alone was responsible for many schools in Wales. The Act of Uniformity was the first legislation to demand subscription to the liturgy by teachers and physicians, and this section was possibly not followed so closely. See Turner, *op. cit.*, III, 65.

30. He sent his request to Bishop Henchman of London, who was asked to send out the orders. See Turner, *op. cit.*, III, 758.

31. The diocesan returns included St. Asaph and St. David in Wales, and Dorset, Bristol, Devon, and Cornwall in England. The records remarkably substantiate Calamy's account (see Turner, *op. cit.*, III, 66). Calamy reported twenty ministers ejected in St. Asaph.

made—the strength of Nonconformity had not been broken. Few Nonconformist ministers had conformed; the Nonconformist laity were still strong, and where they had conformed there was left the doubt of their sincerity. The Conventicle Act, which had been in force only about a year, had undoubtedly strengthened the morale and stiffened resistance and, what was still more serious, had developed a more sympathetic attitude on the part of the Low-Churchmen and many magistrates. When the plague struck London the next year and spread over England, the zeal of the Nonconformist clergy as compared with the Anglican made for them many supporters and friends.

The effort to force Nonconformity had been a complete failure. The three years had purged much of the dross from the Puritan character, had deepened its spiritual nature and emphasized its unselfishness. Moreover, the brief period had made it clear to the Presbyterian element that there was little chance for comprehension and thus had emphasized for them the need of toleration. The sects within the Nonconformist group were unified in spirit and strengthened. From this time there is a rapidly growing number of pamphlets urging the need of toleration—pamphlets from the pens of Presbyterians and Low-Churchmen as well as from those who had long espoused the cause of liberty in religion.[32]

32. The author is indebted to the editor of *Renaissance Studies in Honor of Hardin Craig* (Stanford University, 1942) for permission to use the material making the greater part of this chapter.

III

THE CRISIS OF

PURITANISM

THE ANGLICAN church failed to take to heart the lessons of 1660-1665. The Cavalier Parliament had done all it was asked to do in the way of statutes to destroy Nonconformity. The government had instructed its officials to enforce the laws, the Archbishop of Canterbury had recommended and urged the support of all churchmen in exterminating the stubborn Nonconformists, and for a portion of this period even the Nonconformist ministry, especially among the Presbyterians, had recommended that their flocks should return to the church. Yet by 1665 the Nonconformist ministry had added new names to replace those lost by death. They had become defiant of authority. The civil agents, especially the justices, began to express their dislike of the work imposed upon them, and persecution was always distasteful to many of the churchmen. Archbishop Sheldon with a small following still felt the necessity of extermination and believed that with the aid of the Clarendon Code and the establishment of a class of zealous informers the work could be done. The period following 1665 he proposed to use to test his purpose. The diocese of Canterbury, Sheldon's own, showed some increase in numbers of Nonconformists in the count of 1665. The diocese of St. Asaph in Wales reported no Nonconformists, although it was well known that many

were there.[1] In most cases there was clearly an unwilling-
ness to coöperate in the search.

In London the plague greatly strengthened the leniency
that had been shown in the persecuting activity during 1665.
The Nonconformist ministers quite generally remained in
London during the crisis, and ere long they were preaching
to people both in the churches where, as Pepys says, "many
times they had to clamber over seats to reach the pulpit,"
and in private houses where they had gone to minister to the
sick.

Parliament was called to meet in Oxford in 1666 because
of the London conditions, and here, with the findings of
the survey of 1665 before him, Sheldon was able finally to
separate the Nonconformist ministers from their flocks by
securing passage of the Five Mile Act,[2] which permitted no
Nonconformist minister to reside within five miles of any
borough or city where he had ministered to a congregation
prior to this time. This act was not as effective as one would
suppose since the removal of all ministers from one congregation only established them in closer contact with others,
and its character and severity led to a growing spirit of opposition on the part of Nonconformists, both laymen and ministers.

In London the act was temporarily nullified by the great
fire which swept the old city in 1666. The destruction of
many of the churches quickly disclosed that the spirit of
service was much greater among the Nonconformists than
among the Anglican clergy. The former met in private
houses, in buildings of all sorts, and in some cases built taber-
nacles for service, while the authorities paid them no attention or refused to follow up information about their meetings. In London this condition continued until 1669 when
the Commons, scandalized by the report of great meetings

1. Turner, *Original Records of Early Nonconformity*, III, 43.
2. *Statutes at Large*, collected by William Hawkins, II, pt. 2, 674; hereafter referred to as *Statutes at Large*.

almost adjoining Parliament house, asked the King to issue a declaration toward a stricter execution of the law. This London situation with respect to absent churchmen and much incompetency had its counterpart in many of the dioceses.[3] The results of the scarcity of educated Anglican clergymen in 1662, when they had been called upon to supply the places vacated by the Nonconformist clergy, began to show more clearly by 1665. Aside from many who had applied for the sake of the living and had no interest in their work except collecting their income, there were many others who, though sincere, were unfit because of lack of education, and the many problems arising in the reconstruction of the church gave little opportunity for remedying this condition. Sheldon's serious effort to overcome this clerical unfitness resulted in the eventual limitation of ordination to those with university education, but the loss of so much of the church's revenues made it impossible to solve the problem. Much the same failure was seen among the London churches. Parliament was asked for funds from time to time, but it had many demands, and in spite of every effort a very general union of parishes had to be made to supplement the work along other lines. During 1667-1668 every effort possible was made to destroy Puritanism. The jails were full to overflowing.[4] Fines grew heavier as the informers demanded their reward. The Quakers made no effort to conceal their services and furnished the majority of the jail population. The Nonconformists became wary and fought back. Meeting places were supplied with an extra door for the pastor's escape. Informers were beaten and guard was kept over entrances to meeting places. In some places the enemies of Nonconformity were overawed, and the business of informer became danger-

3. *Calendar of State Papers, Venetian,* 1666-1669, p. 655; *Debates of the House of Commons,* collected by Anchitel Grey, I, 175; hereafter referred to as Grey, *Debates.*

4. Grey, *Debates,* I, 104 ff.; Anon., *A Few Sober Queries upon the late Proclamation for Enforcing Laws against Conventicles.*

ous to life and limb.[5] But most of the justices refused to
act as long as possible, and sympathy for the sufferers was
too strong to be overcome.

In many dioceses the bishops were opposed to persecution,
sometimes freeing the culprit after conviction and often
sharing his income to succor the persecuted. In a few
bishoprics the archbishop was given full support and the
bishop took the lead in persecuting both clergy and laity.
Ward of the bishopric of Exeter, Gunning of Chichester, together with Sheldon of Canterbury, were most active. In
these three bishoprics the greatest use was made of informers; with the bishops' urging, the civil authorities were generally zealous, and consequently the suffering was great. Yet
in Canterbury Sheldon found that Nonconformity was growing[6] both in numbers and boldness, while in the other two
dioceses the numbers were still large, as disclosed by the
arrest of ministers and laity. In 1667 the first Conventicle
Act, effective for five years, came to its end, and while other
acts were enforcible, there was a general easing of persecution until 1670 when the act was not only renewed but was
made more severe.

The period of 1667-1670 was given over to a lively pamphlet debate while Parliament wrestled, against a strong opposition, with the Conventicle Act. There is to be found a new
type of pamphlet which calls attention to the growing evil
of the kingdom—swearing, intemperance, unfaithfulness—
and ascribes the increasing irreligion to the religious troubles.
Many ask for comprehension and all for a broader toleration.
A growing number of Presbyterians as well as some Low-
Churchmen were urging toleration as the only possible solution of the trouble.[7]

There is also a new note to be found in many of the pamphlets calling attention to the economic depression of the

5. *Calender of State Papers, Venetian*, 1667, from June to September.
6. Turner, *op. cit.*, III, Introduction.
7. Samuel Pepys, *Diary*, VII, 46 ff., 323 ff.

period and relating it to the persecutions of the Nonconformists, who were declared to be the economic backbone of the
country.   Commerce was on the wane, while a rapid growth
of unemployment, of resultant crime, and a general weakening of the economic structure called for a more lenient
treatment of Nonconformity on the ground that it should
not be the business of the state to support a religious organization.[8]

The general hardships of the period following the great
fire gave a new turn to the religious problem.   London was
sure that the King was bent on alleviating the conditions
under which Nonconformity was laboring, either for the sake
of the Catholics or because of a disaffection toward the
bishops.[9]   Conditions at the court never had seemed so bad
"for gaming, swearing, whoring, drinking and the most
abominable vices that ever were in the world."[10]   The act
of 1666 forced the Nonconformists to fight, so that the
bishops were greatly concerned with the lenient disposition
of the court,[11] and there was a tendency to shift the blame
to the court.[12] The most telling pamphlets, however, stressed
the effects of persecution upon industry and order.

Thus, while in a few dioceses persecution was greatly advanced and strengthened, in most parts the worst stage of
both the church and state activity had slackened for the
moment.   The Low-Church leaders were bolder and more
active, and were strongly in favor of relaxing the laws.   In
1667 there was a conference between the moderate churchmen, Stillingfleet and Tillotson, and the Presbyterians, Baxter, Calamy and Manton, though no results appeared.[13]
Several pamphlets by Low-Church authors stressed the need

8. *Ibid.*, p. 332.
9. *Ibid.*, p. 323 (January, 1667).
10. *Ibid.*, VIII, 39 (January, 1667).
11. Richard Allestree, *Causes of the Decay of Christian Piety.*
12. Pepys, *Diary*, VII, 256 (July 1667).
13. John Richard Green, *History of the English People*, III, 394.   The
archbishop's advice caused them to drop the matter.

of peace and united effort to combat the evils of the time, while laymen also became vocal in the interests of comprehension and toleration.[14]

In Parliament, too, most of these ideas were aired. The fall of Clarendon gave new hope to the Nonconformists. Legislation was introduced looking toward the enactment of a law to restore the Puritan Sabbath, toward stricter control of morals, as well as an unwelcome effort toward comprehension. On the other hand the Anglicans were successful in securing passage of a press act to supervise the pamphlet criticism of church and government, in forcing the King's hand to further the execution of the laws, and in renewing the Conventicle Act. This was a long fight, for not until 1670 was the renewal act passed, although there was almost continuous debate on the matter. The House was more ready to take action against the Catholics, and Charles was required to order them from London; later, 1673, the Test Act was presented to him, which in the minds of most legislators was intended to drive the Catholics from office; however, it affected Nonconformists in the same way except that, having been used to attending service and communion, they found it no hardship.

During the period 1667-1670, when the bill for the renewal of the Conventicle Act was before Parliament, there was an ever-increasing complaint from churchmen of the growing numbers of Nonconformists, of the lack of secular support in enforcing the laws, of the boldness of the dissidents, while in the debates in Parliament there were complaints of the sparseness of church attendance, of a dangerous alteration of doctrine and service in the efforts to draw the people to the services. On the other hand, it was argued that the severity of the laws was stultifying commerce and weakening the nation's strength.[15]

14. Allestree, *op. cit.*; A. L. Littleton, *The Church's Peace Asserted on a Civil Account*; Simon Patrick, *The Parable of the Pilgrim*.
15. Grey, *Debates*, I, 104, 127-28, 144, 246.

There was much pamphlet discussion which drew the attention of the Venetian ambassador. In this pamphlet war, the opposition to the bill was well presented. One of the strongest opponents of the bill sent to the King a pamphlet in which he argued that such a measure was opposed to all Christian principles and was urged only by the bishops. That the bill was mainly to protect England from plots, the bishops knew was false since any meeting could be entered and would be always open if persecution eased. He contended that plots against the government were laid in the coffee houses and taverns and completed in private houses; that even the Turk had better sense than to enact such laws. He warned the King that if he failed the Nonconformists in this matter, he would never regain their confidence and that the nation needed a united people. Foreign affairs demanded this, and the economic conditions demanded it. The King, he urged, should know that the sympathy of the laity was so general as to make execution of the law difficult or impossible.[16] It was a calm and reasoned pamphlet, and its arguments were supported by a conference of Presbyterian and Independent ministers who agreed to forget comprehension and ask the King for a complete toleration. At the same time a petition was presented to the King by sixty master clothworkers together with 20,000 workmen asking for a toleration of the Nonconformist to aid their commerce.[17]

By 1670 Charles was too pressed for funds to oppose Parliament too far. When Parliament withheld the funds until the King accepted the measure, he not only signed it but for the moment urged the government to aid the churchmen in its enforcement.[18] By this time, however, the council was

16. *Ibid.*, p. 670; Anon., *A Few Sober Queries upon the late Proclamation.* A very fine and sober list of queries by a Nonconformist.

17. *Calendar of State Papers, Venetian,* 1669-1670, p. 84. This seems to have been the point, July, 1669, when many Presbyterians gave way and advocated toleration as the way out.

18. The secretary of the Privy Council, Williamson, was especially active during this period.

divided.   The by-elections were steadily increasing the number of members opposed to the government, while local officials generally had little stomach for the work.   There is a
steady complaint by churchmen from this time of the laxness
of the enforcement of the laws against Nonconformity.[19]

In 1669 Archbishop Sheldon, perhaps to aid passage of the
new Conventicle Act, ordered a new survey of the kingdom
to determine the numbers and character of the Nonconformist body.[20]   This survey is the most complete and valuable that we have for any determination as to the effectiveness of the policy of suppression, and while incomplete
enough to make definite statements impossible, yet it does
enable the student to draw some valuable conclusions as to
the real effectiveness of the persecution.

Sheldon's order was explicit.   He wanted information upon
the Nonconformist ministry and concerning the known conventicles with number of attendance, and character and standing of the laity.   He wanted information as to the assistance
rendered by the secular authorities and whether such assistance rendered the task of the survey more complete and satisfactory.   There seem to have been additional private instructions; Bishop Kennet remarks that among these was one to
make the reports show numbers as small as possible.   The
conditions, social and economic, of the Nonconformists were
asked for and were given very freely: "They [Friends]
live in adultry"; "Mean, very poor"; "A middling sort with
a few gentry"; "Mere tradesmen"; "Pretty good estates";
"Of five hundred pounds, some two hundred or one hundred
pounds and some sixty pounds." As to the clergy, the report
shows that "they were moving about, many new ones, un-
educated [among Friends and Anabaptists] and maintain
themselves in trade."[21]

As to the returns, five of the English dioceses have left

19. *Calendar of State Papers, Venetian*, 1669-1670, pp. 152-53.
20. Turner, *op. cit.*, III, note to Pt. I, Ch. I.   The returns are so
scanty as to be tantalizing.   21. *Ibid.*, pp. 76-77.

no returns and one Welsh diocese is missing. In a number
of the others only a part of the diocese is given and in several,
single counties are missing. Two bishops, Ward, lately transferred to Sarum, and Gunning of Chichester, give the most
complete returns. Ward's would be invaluable had he not
in the latter part of 1667 been transferred to Sarum from
Exeter, where he had given a full return in 1665.

Sheldon, in his report to the council on the survey, suggests hopefully that "probably many are duplicates as attending two conventicles and that probably they are mostly women and children."[22] It is interesting to note that the de-
creased numbers are more striking in the dioceses least fully
reported,[23] which suggests that there the archbishop's instructions to make the numbers small was kept most clearly in
mind.

The report revealed some 120,000 to 123,000 Presbyterians and Independents with 1,138 teachers, 1,234 conventicles and 907 houses where meetings were held.[24] The
diocese of Somerset recorded the largest number of both
ministers and laymen, with London a close second. The
numbers decrease as one goes farther from London, except
in the Southwest, which, like the diocese of Canterbury, was
very strong and rather defiant.[25] It is quite clear that the
reports can in no sense be complete and are an underesti-
mate of the numbers, which appear to be in the proportion
of one to ten of the population.[26] Many of the older ministers continued to urge their adherents to attend the conformist services, to take communion (church communion was
the test for conformity), and to supplement these observ-
ances by home services. In very many places the execution
of the law remained lax, and many conventicles and ministers
were merely winked at and probably not reported. Two

22. *Ibid.,* p. 804. It should be kept in mind that the reports given
counted only children over sixteen years of age.
23. *Ibid.,* p. 78.   24. *Ibid.,* p. 114.
25. *Ibid.,* p. 120.   26. *Ibid.,* p. 123.

years later when the indulgence was issued, while many
Presbyterians and Independents hesitated to ask for them
lest they encourage the toleration of Catholics, yet Presbyterian licenses reached something over 2,500, with about
1,100 Independents and with Baptists over 400.[27]

The report on the whole must have been a great disappointment to the archbishop. It probably aided materially
by this very disappointment in forcing through Parliament
a renewed Conventicle Act and of making it much more
severe than the earlier one, though the Lords forced an
amendment largely freeing the nobility from its execution.
The penalties, fifty pounds for a minister and ten pounds
for attendants at service, defeated the law in large part, for
the authorities refused to execute it. After less than a year
the King came to the conclusion that an indulgence could be
applied, so with the consent of most of his council, Shaftesbury not participating, he issued it, March 15, 1672. He
seems to have been convinced by the strong wave of opposition to the enforcement of the act of 1670 and by the belief
that, with the Dutch war in the offing, enforcement might
lead to political intrigue.

In how far he meant it to be an easement of the Catholic
persecution must remain unanswered, but it is certain that
there was much hesitation on the part of the Presbyterian
group lest this be the real purpose of the indulgence. This
led Charles to explain carefully, too carefully, perhaps, to
Parliament that the indulgence gave the Catholics no more
liberty than before, which was true, but suspicion remained
strong. Neither Buckingham nor Shaftesbury, the strongest
supporters of Nonconformity, gave any support to the indulgence; yet they did not oppose it, and the political opposition were active in attacking it, principally on the basis that
it was a step toward indulging the Catholic party.

27. *Ibid.*, pp. 726 ff. With the population this would mean about
500,000 Nonconformists. The majority of the houses registered for meetings were those of the aristocracy. See Turner's list.

As time passed, however, the Nonconformists decided that they might as well accept the King's offer. Not many came to Whitehall to ask for the document, but soon men appeared for friends, and within a few months some 4,222 licenses had been issued for ministers or for houses for worship.[28] Of these there were 2,583 Presbyterian teachers or householders, 1,183 Independents, 412 Baptists. The Friends refused to make application.[29]

The activity of the Indulgence Office in Whitehall supplies something of a check on the diocesan reports of 1669. It is clear proof that the reports had emphasized the effects of the persecution upon the decrease of numbers and that Nonconformity had not only held its own but had been strengthened. Both Anglican and Nonconformist asserted that large numbers flocked to the new preaching,[30] and the diocesan report from Canterbury showed double the number of Nonconformists in the diocese by 1676.[31]

The indulgence granted freedom of worship and of preaching, and declared for cessation of persecution, so that the Friends who refused indulgence as well as those Nonconformists who hesitated or neglected to ask for a license were not interfered with. When Bishop Ward in Sarum continued to hunt those without license, the King sent word to him to desist.[32] For one year there was religious peace in England.

When Parliament met in 1673, however, the storm broke. The Dutch war was opening, but the House was interested only in the Declaration of Indulgence. The King told them he did not intend to give way, but they insisted that the King might not nullify an act of Parliament by a declaration. This position of the House gave Sheldon his chance to force the withdrawal of the declaration and when Charles found he could get no funds he gave way and issued a proclamation

28. *Ibid.*, p. 714; cf. p. 156.
29. *Ibid.*, p. 731.   30. *Ibid.*, p. 147.
31. *Ibid.*, p. 804.   32. *Ibid.*, p. 148.

withdrawing the indulgence.[33]   However, the House made it clear that they were not so incensed against the declaration as against the King's illegal act and intimated that they would legislate to meet Nonconformist wishes.[34]   During 1673 an act passed both houses of Parliament, but prorogation came prior to agreement on all its terms.[35]

However, the King's action for the time brought to an end any successful attack upon Nonconformity. When the indulgence was withdrawn, many of those holding licenses refused to accept the withdrawal as more than disallowing a renewal of the license and continued preaching and meetings. The courts were either undecided as to the legal status or took advantage of the situation and in most cases refused to convict, so that while persecution continued, its effectiveness was dulled.

In 1675 came a strong renewal of efforts toward toleration. The Duke of Buckingham offered a bill in the House of Lords basing its need wholly on economic grounds and the unity and strength of the nation. The bill failed but revealed a strong Nonconformist sympathy in Parliament.[36]   The Low-Church group renewed a conference with Baxter, Calamy, Manton, and others, but the bishops' opposition again broke off the conference.[37] A number of Anglican pamphlets appeared in 1675 arguing for peace in religious affairs for the sake of avoiding the greater danger of the Catholic menace.[38]   Many lay pamphlets especially emphasized the economic side of the controversy.   There was little argu-

33. *Ibid.*, p. 245.
34. Grey, *Debates*, 1672; House *Journals*, 1672.
35. *Lords Journals*, 1673, p. 280.
36. Both houses were inclined toward tolerance, but the bishops balked agreement in the Lords. See H. M. C., *Portland MSS.*, III, 349.
37. Edward Cardwell, *Documentary Annals of the Reformed Church of England*, II, 288-89; Turner, *op. cit.*, III, 58.
38. Herbert Croft, *The Naked Truth* (published anonymously). Bishop Croft and William Sherlock argued the matter on the inconsiderable number of Nonconformists (see Turner, *op. cit.*, III, 59; H. M. C., *Portland MSS.*, III, 349).

ment as to method but a strong feeling as to the end desired,[39] which was more severity toward Catholics and some definite easing of Protestant persecution.

The period 1666-1675 was a really decisive one in religious affairs and in political affairs as well. The strength of Anglicanism in Parliament had become greatly weakened, a strong opposition had come into being which both sympathized with Nonconformity and saw an advantage in supporting it on occasion, and clearly recognized that the country had tired of the Church's efforts at persecution. The rapid development of the trade with Holland had strongly emphasized the economic phase of the problem, and the prominence of the Catholic question abroad gave the party a strong handle for opposition and greatly added to its strength.

There had also developed a very general lay opposition to continued persecution. The passing of time had divorced Nonconformity from its supposed alliance with the Commonwealth, and this supposed relationship was always one of the strongest arguments for persecution. Even the church could see that the purpose of the persecution had failed when the indulgence brought into the open so large an increase in the numbers of those who, as persecution ceased, were ready to identify themselves with the movement, and especially when it revealed so many sympathizers among the aristocracy.[40] Many of the more earnest churchmen testified that the effects of the persecution could be seen in the weakening of the spirituality of the church itself, and from then on a much greater effort was made to combat wickedness in high places, to put more emphasis upon the very purposes for which Nonconformity had fought—the sacredness of the Sabbath,

39. The arguments extend from comprehension to complete toleration of Protestants and to the ignoring of religious matters by the state. (Many of the pamphlets are found in the Union Theological Library and in the Seligman Collection in the Columbia University Library.)

40. Mr. Turner has disclosed that most of the houses registered for meetings under the indulgence were those of the aristocracy.

cleanness of life, the individual character of the Christian life, and the sacredness of the personality of the individual. Not that Nonconformists were yet to have their way, but their number was increasing as was the need for greater unity to combat the King's intention to have *his* way, and many voices were being raised to turn attention away from Nonconformity to more important problems.

In a very practical sense the period brought out at certain points that opposition to the King's arbitrary power, which during the Long Parliament had united Nonconformist, Anglican Puritan, and Constitutionalist against Charles I. The formation of a Whig party[41] in opposition to the Tory marks the point where the leadership against arbitrary authority of the Crown passed from the religious Puritan to the upholders of English common law and to the authority of Parliament as representatives of the nation, a point clearly expressed by the Convention Parliament in its assertion that government must be by King, Lords, and Commons. It was unfortunate that in this division into parties the Anglicans should have again asserted the absolute powers of the King and allied themselves against the clearly forming national mind.

41. After 1672 the King came to feel strongly that the Whig party at its roots represented the Nonconformist party. He counted Buckingham and Shaftesbury as the leaders of all who opposed him, and, as trouble with Parliament grew, he announced that his efforts must be to destroy Nonconformity.

IV

THE CRISIS OF

NONCONFORMITY

THE FAILURE of Charles's plan for an indulgence seems to have been the turning point in his attitude toward Nonconformity. The organization of the opposition in Parliament, its insistence that the Declaration of Indulgence, being an unconstitutional act, must be withdrawn before a discussion of funds was begun, exasperated him. The efforts to implicate him in the charge of papal interest probably hastened his decision to change his course. This was first given voice when Parliament was prorogued on the eve of agreement to a measure designed to give relief to Nonconformists by law instead of through the King's declaration. The preceding session of Parliament in 1670-1671 had begun the discussion of a bill to exclude Catholics from office,[1] and the succeeding session seemed prepared to push this bill to completion. The implication was clear that Parliament thought Charles's indulgence was meant to ease the situation for Catholics.[2] The Presbyterian Puritans had hesitated to ask for the indulgence because of the general feeling that it was

1. *House Journals*, February 23, 1670, p. 207. This was replaced by an address against popery which passed both houses and was presented to the King (see p. 549).

2. The Venetian ambassador reported that there was a general feeling that the King intended to revive popery (*Calendar of State Papers, Venetian*, 1671-1672, p. 226); also that Charles meant it to prepare a way to destroy Parliament's power, and even the Catholics feared Charles's purpose (p. 226).

meant to aid the Catholic cause. This idea was very prevalent, as the Venetian reports indicated.

In a discussion of the bill in 1670 and 1671 to exclude
Catholics from office, the House had quickly voted down a
provision to include the Nonconformists. The by-elections
of the preceding period had consistently gone against the
Tory party, and Nonconformists were favoring the Whig
party in the elections. As a matter of fact, the indulgence
was the chief event that united Nonconformity, that is, the
struggle for religious liberty, with the larger struggle for
constitutional and economic liberty, because of the greater
general opposition to the Catholic interests. The issues
raised by the indulgence recalled the struggle of the Long
Parliament which united religious and constitutional forces
to check the power of the King. As in 1640, it brought the
Low-Churchman slowly yet inevitably to join the forces of
opposition by the suspicion of its relation to the Catholic
question.

If Charles was not from the beginning convinced that
the time would come to restore the Catholic faith in England, at least from this time forward he was sure that he
could get no support from the group he had tried to befriend,
while some of the leading Catholics among the aristocracy
came to his support.[3] The immediate result was to cause
many Low-Churchmen hitherto Tories to unite with the
Whigs in 1673 to force the Test Act upon the King, and he
was persuaded to sign the bill and to dismiss the Catholics
from his council.[4]

When Parliament met in 1675, the Lord Keeper, Finch,
suggested that since the King had withdrawn the indulgence
and accepted the Test Act depriving the Catholics of any
position under the government, Parliament would do well

3. *Ibid.*, p. 226. The suggestion had been made that the Whig party
was but the Parliament group of Nonconformists and their sympathizers
(see Anthony Ashley Cooper, *A Letter from a Parliament Man to his
Friend*).   4. Grey, *Debates*, II, 196 ff.

to give some attention to the needs of the Anglican church.[5] Much complaint had been made of the weaknesses, ineffectiveness and laxness of the church. The King was urging a house cleaning and desired the participation of Parliament. There was some discussion. Parliament recommended more frequent convocations and better support of parish priests, vicars, and curates, but was too engrossed in other matters to give the church troubles any real attention.

The Declaration to withdraw the licenses in 1673 brought a renewal of persecution. For a time the holders fought for their certificates, and the courts hesitated to enforce the law in the face of these permits, probably because they did not know the King's mind. The church was especially troubled because during the period of indulgence large numbers had flocked to the Nonconformist churches[6] so that through 1673-1674 the church assumed the initiative in persecution, sometimes with, and more often without, help from the laity. It was a comparatively mild period since but few bishops' favored persecution. Ward in Salisbury, Rainbow in Carlisle, the bishops of Durham and York, and the diocesan authorities of Canterbury were bitterly busy but none too effective; Morley in London was very lenient,[7] and when in the course of affairs Baxter, Manton, and Howe were arrested, he offered his services to free them. The justices, however, refused the evidence of the informers and they were quickly set at liberty, as were others in London, and the informers were fined.[8]

London probably suffered least in this period, although there was much feeling among churchmen against the bishops

5. *Lords Journals*, 1675, pp. 4, 30-33; Charles II, *His Majesty's gracious Speech, together with the Lord Keeper's to both Houses of Parliament, April 13, 1675*; W. D. B., *A Letter to the Right Worshipful T. S.*; R. Hart, *Parish Churches turned into Conventicles.*

6. The Anglicans in many places complained that their churches were drained of worshipers under the indulgence.

7. Turner, *op. cit.*, III, 104 ff.

8. *Ibid.*, 38; H. M. C., *Portland MSS.*, III, 349.

for failure to aid the law enforcers, who were mainly informers.[9] The many complaints seem to have induced Bishop Morley to suggest to the King another review of Nonconformist numbers, and in 1676 Archbishop Sheldon finally took the initiative in giving instructions to the bishops for such a survey. This last count before the Revolution, except for a few places, seems to have been very perfunctory. Ward in Salisbury made a very detailed search which, if it had been comparable with that of 1669, would have been greatly worth while, but the report from Salisbury at the earlier date was merely a general statement, so there could be no comparison. The returns of 1676 found the Nonconformists strongest in the archbishop's own diocese of Canterbury where it is possible the work was done most carefully. On the whole there were fewer reports than in 1665, so far as they have been found.[10] Only Canterbury and Salisbury[11] gave satisfactory returns; York and Winchester gave summaries, and, the rest seem to have ignored the request or the reports are lost. The archbishop made nothing of the survey except to urge stronger persecution, although it was clear in his own diocese that the Nonconformists had increased and were prepared to defend themselves.[12] With other matters engaging public attention, the year 1677 passed by with certainly no additional hardships for Nonconformists.[13] The effort to count heads brought out clearly the

9. In Chester especially there was continuous and bitter complaint. See Turner, *op. cit.*, III, 146; *Calendar of State Papers, Domestic*, 1676-1678, correspondence of L'Estrange with Williamson, secretary of the Privy Council.

10. These returns are in the William Salt Public Reference Library at Stafford (see Turner, *op. cit.*, III, 140).

11. Ward's chief assistant reported, however, that many Nonconformists returned to church for the count.

12. In Canterbury the returns showed one in nine to be Nonconformists, and in London, one in twelve (see Turner, *op. cit.*, III, 143). Sheldon died in 1677, which may account for this survey being so quickly forgotten.

13. The Dutch war was not going well, and there were rumors of a Catholic plot in Ireland, probably false (see Turner, *op. cit.*, III, 38).

fact that there were many Nonconformists who found it easy to return to the church when danger appeared and that England on the whole was tired of persecution. Even during 1677 there was an increase of pamphlet material directed against the Catholics and criticising the Anglican church for dividing Protestantism in the face of the papal efforts. When in 1678 the so-called Catholic plot made its appearance, Non-conformity, being anti-Catholic, had a period of almost complete rest from persecution.

During 1678 to 1680 pamphlet material was very largely directed against the "Catholic danger," but the feeling was not at all unanimous. Some writers blamed the Church of England for its rise, charging that many churchmen favored the Catholics as against the Nonconformists because of the similarity in the ritual and service, while the conformist clergy as a whole had strengthened its growth through inattention to religious matters because of sympathy with popery and of hostility to the Puritans.[14] Some Anglicans were suspicious, as was the King, that the Nonconformists were guilty of the plot and wished only to turn attention from themselves; at the same time many secular pamphlets condemned the church for concentrating attention against those whose consciences refused to allow them to conform while encouraging popery as well as all the other evils of the time.

With the turmoil occasioned by the Catholic plot behind him, Charles II devoted the remaining years of his reign to a stern and unrelenting administration of the laws pertaining to religion, instructing all officials under severe penalty to give full attention to the problem. From 1681 the government through the Privy Council tried to enforce the laws. Charles remarked to Gilbert Burnet that now he intended to

14. William Dell, *The Increase of Popery in England* (prepared in 1667 but seized in press and not published until 1681); Anon., *The Reformed Papist and High Churchman*; J. Nalson, *A Letter from a Jesuit in Paris to his correspondent in London.*

settle matters with Nonconformity. He was induced to this by the belief that the Puritan was the backbone of the Whig party and its destruction would make his plans the more feasible.

The secretary of home affairs, urged on by the King's council, put his agents everywhere and a continuous stream of correspondence flowed through the office of Williamson, the secretary of the council. Charles readily supplied the proclamation for increased violence, and Archbishop Sancroft in full sympathy laid upon the parish ecclesiastical authorities the responsibility of aiding in every way possible. Both clergy and laity came under restraint. Brought for the first time into the ecclesiastical courts, where conviction was certain, the pastors were both fined and imprisoned, their goods were seized, and their property was sold, while the Elizabethan law was invoked against the laity, and twenty pounds per month was levied for non-attendance at the parish church.

In Bristol alone, Luttrell notices that the authorities expected to collect £100,000 during a single year and hesitated only when the jails could hold no more offenders.[15] In 1682, Captain Hilton, described as the captain of the informers, wrote to the council that in six months he had convicted Nonconformists to the value of £17,000 and "had so many agents he could not support them."[16] Defoe asserted that 8,000 Nonconformists had perished in prison during the reign of Charles II,[17] while Penn in 1687 declared that 15,000 had died for conscience' sake.[18] Jeremy White later made a list of the Nonconformists who had been prosecuted under Charles II and found the number to be 60,000, while

15. Narcissus Luttrell, *A Brief Historical Relation of State Affairs;* Vol. I gives repeated accounts of the severity of persecution, 1681 to 1685.
16. *Calendar of State Papers, Domestic,* 1682, p. 521.
17. See Defoe's Preface to Delaume's *Plea for the Nonconformists* added to the seventh reprinting (1706). The *Plea* was first printed in 1684.
18. William Penn, *Good Advice to the Church of England,* cited by Whiting, *Studies in English Puritanism, 1660-1688,* p. 440.

5,000 had died in prison.[19] The economic losses of the Puritans of the period were estimated at from £2,000,000 to £12,-
000,000 or £14,000,000.[20] But the increasing complaints of
economic losses through arrests and fear of arrests make the
estimated sums seem fairly reasonable. Many small traders
emigrated to the Continent and America, and Neal cites
churches in Amsterdam, Rotterdam, Utrecht, Leyden, and
elsewhere that were made up of the refugees.[21] In the light
of Turner's findings, especially in the 1669 returns, these
figures seem very conservative, for it must be kept in mind,
as the churchmen stated from time to time, that the severe
persecution and the attempts to count numbers brought many
Nonconformists to church for short periods, only to drop
away when the crisis was over. Churchmen had complained
that Charles's indulgence in 1672 emptied the churches and
filled the conventicles and now again, during the savage persecutions of 1681 to 1685, the Nonconformist leaders advised
their adherents to attend their parish churches and occasionally to take communion.

By 1685 the jails were filled to overflowing. James II's
accession found 5,000 Quakers in prison. The other sects
were more wary, but they as well as the Quakers went to
prison and suffered in fines or fled abroad. The Nonconformists clearly recognized their great danger and fought
back as best they could. Money was found with which to
fight arrests. Opinions given by the legal profession denied
the legality of the methods used.[22] The Habeas Corpus
Act was invoked to free prisoners, and the government was
made to fight the cases where possible; this largely nullified any profit. The informers arrested for falsifying evidence were petitioning the government for protection.

19. Whiting, *op. cit.*, p. 440.   20. *Ibid.*, p. 441.
21. Daniel Neal, *History of the Puritans*, Vol. II, Ch. X; see also
Whiting, *op. cit.*, p. 441.
22. Edward Whitaker, *An Answer to the Middlesex Justices dated the
twentieth December last touching the Suppressing of Conventicles*; Anon.,
A Letter from a Justice of the Peace to a Counsellor at Law.

The intelligent Anglican laity generally sympathized with and aided the persecuted. Noblemen protected them from the informers and gave them shelter from law or paid their fines, sometimes the fines of a whole congregation. There was a growing feeling among the Anglican laity and the moderate churchmen that the real struggle was one between the Roman church and Protestantism, which left no time for quarrels among the Protestants. A member of the old Parliament declared that this persecution was especially dangerous as an attempt to strengthen the King's prerogative over the law rather than through the law, and that the church should recognize that its aid would prove its own ruin.[23]

The addition of the political reason for persecution made the period far more savage in its punishments than formerly. Through the by-elections as well as by the wisdom engendered through experience, the Whig party had grown so strong by 1676 as to defeat the King's purpose, so that by 1681 both High-Churchmen and King assumed that the destruction of the Nonconformists would restore the Cavalier party to its older sympathy with and subservience to the King and council. This seems to have been partly the King's motive in the withdrawal of the charters, since wherever the Tory became supreme, the charter was at once given up to be rewritten to exclude the opposition Whig and Nonconformist group. The change of method in persecution seems to have been based upon the desire to destroy the economic and political prominence of well-to-do Nonconformists. The cases were largely drawn to the ecclesiastical courts where excommunication followed the fines exacted under the old Elizabethan acts, as well as imprisonment of all convicted of attendance at a conventicle or absence from church service for a month. Since excommunication was effective in destroying

23. See a broadside publication of a speech in Chester by Henry Booth on his election to the Parliament of 1681 (London, 1681); Privy Council Registers, June 1680 to May 1683.

the civil freedom and political rights of the individual, conviction thus deprived a voter and possible office holder of his exercise of these rights.

It must be concluded, however, that the severities of the period together with the weightiness of the political questions at issue, as in 1641 and 1642, had brought to the support of the Nonconformists many of the bishops, the major part of the intelligent Low-Church laity, who were sympathetic with the sufferers, a very large proportion of the trading classes, who deprecated the economic losses to the nation, and the greater number of those who again saw the supreme issue to be the arbitrary power of the King, while most churchmen as well as laymen saw the danger looming of Roman influence. During 1678 and 1679 Charles was particularly careful in his dealings with Parliament lest fear of the Catholics drive Parliament and the nation to extremities. As to the succession, he early suggested that if Parliament could find a way to curb satisfactorily the power of a Catholic king, he would accept the plan and would promise that James should agree with it; but he refused to submit to James's exclusion and later was only saved from this demand of Parliament through the efforts of Halifax, who, although he was opposed to the Catholics as well as to the persecution of Nonconformists, yet refused to exclude James and persuaded enough of the peers to defeat the final bill in the upper house. Charles thus had the satisfaction of seeing the exclusion bill fail without his direct intervention, and when Parliament presented a bill to relieve the Nonconformist, he saw to it that the measure was mislaid and was not presented for his acceptance when Parliament was dissolved.[24]

In spite of the strict censorship, this period, 1681-1685, produced an abundance of Nonconformist pamphlets. Baxter,

24. Gilbert Burnet, *History of His Own Time*, II, 1-2. Neal in his *History of the Puritans* cites Burnet but goes into some detail in the matter. The evidence from the *Lords Journals* seems to confirm Neal's account; see also Luttrell, *op. cit.*, I, 63.

who was now residing in London, kept his pen busy, and some half dozen pamphlets, explanatory and defensive, from his pen made their appearance. In 1679, in answer to Stillingfleet's sermon in the House of Lords charging no necessity for refusing conformity, he wrote the noblest defense of the Nonconformist principles and reasons for toleration that is to be found during the entire period.[25] He reviewed the efforts made by the friends of religion on both sides of the controversy and emphasized the Christian spirit in which the Nonconformist generally had taken his persecution. He finally laid the greater blame for conditions on a small faction of the high Anglicans who persistently refused any conciliation except abject surrender, which he declared impossible. There is seen in this pamphlet a much greater respect for the sects. Although Baxter still urged comprehension, he made a careful distinction between Protestant Nonconformists and Catholics while showing regard for the religious tenets of the Catholic church as opposed to its organization and policy. There is a fine statement of what the life of the layman should be and what should be the ideal of the minister. Altogether it was conciliatory, honest, without prejudice, and it must have had a good influence upon all who were prepared to see that the problem was one which time had proved could not be solved by penal laws and persecution.

The period may also be said to have largely erased the distinction between comprehension and toleration. To be sure, Baxter almost alone still maintained the former in the back of his mind, but generally there was a growing unity of the sects, and distinction was now drawn between the dissenting Protestant and the Catholic. There was much more discussion of the evil effects of controversy upon religion generally and the presence of great evils to which the church should

25. Richard Baxter, *The Nonconformist Plea for Peace.* The Baxter pamphlets of the period are all found in the McAlpin collection in Union Theological Library, New York.

give its attention.   In 1677 Parliament passed the law on
Sunday observance with little diversity of opinion, and in
1675, W. D. B. sent a letter to T. S. calling attention to the
effect of severe legal restraints in religion which breed contempt for law and for the ruler and tend "to depopulate the
country and lessen the revenues and trade."   The church
should depend upon instruction.   "Not one in ten thousand
have read the thirty-nine articles" and the differences generally are not vital.   The church had best want some truths
than to have no peace, and there is much in the church that
needs reform, W. D. B. continued.   "We have 9000 benefices
and thirty thousand admitted to Holy Orders so that most
have no subsistence. The benefices are enjoyed by five thousand persons who largely officiate through ignorant, and
sometimes scandalous and debauched persons interested only
in their living not their work.   For this reason our churches
are empty and the work of the Nonconformist well done."[26]

Even many of the strong defenders of the church, Low-
Churchmen usually, were moved to caution her upon her own
shortcomings, to advise reformation as the best support
against both papist and Nonconformist, and to decry persecution, since the greater part of the nation was out of sympathy with it and utterly opposed to the informer system.
Even "the generality of the country gentry . . . profess as
great an abhorence to persecution as they have for depopu-
lating the countries."[27]   "I think there is not one party in
England that holds it as a principle of their religion that
it is lawful to persecute for mere religion."[28]   The Quaker
who in these later days was modest and accepted quietly the
prison and loss of property had gone far to bring the people
to see the folly of persecution.[29]

26. W. D. B., *A Letter from a Churchman to the Right Worshipful
T. S.*
27. Anon., *A Letter from a Gentleman in the City to a Gentleman in
the Country about the Odiousness of Persecution.*   28. *Ibid.*, pp. 14-15.
29. *Ibid.*, pp. 21-22.   This pamphlet was brought to the attention of
Parliament and ordered burned.

There is also in these pamphlets a clear recognition of the growing danger of papal influence, and already by 1678 the English mind had been prepared for the popish plot. For some months there was a very general readiness to believe any charge against the Catholics, and while Charles was certainly skeptical, he was loath to oppose the popular mind. His careful interference with the judges during the preceding period to enable the government to control the courts only made the matter worse, for in hunting out the plotters, the same judges were ready to accept any and all evidence of any character.

The determined and changed attitude of Charles after 1679 was not lost on the Nonconformists and this fact may have had some influence upon their literature. Few Nonconformists were prepared openly to defy the government, hence the greater part of their literature carried a tone of distinct conciliation and was passed by the censor. It was an effort to make church and government comprehend that Nonconformity was quite separate from all political plots and was interested only in religious liberty and the welfare of the state.

In 1680 a pamphlet[30] attempted to make clear the tenets and purpose of the Presbyterian Puritan group. It declared that the Presbyterians were the logical successors of early Puritanism. They accepted the Scriptures first as a general guide of religious affairs and had never opposed the government of King and Parliament. They believed that in religion the Scriptures should be the rule of faith and worship, that man should be given latitude in his reading and interpretation, that man's conscience was the final arbiter of his faith when he had honestly studied the Scriptures, and that the whole history of English Presbyterianism had shown the Presbyterian to be consistent in this effort. The Presbyterian Puritan had never been found disloyal to the govern-

30. Anon., *English Presbytery: an Account of the Main Opinions.*

ment, nor had he opposed the Anglican state church. This general statement was followed closely by Baxter in a later pamphlet[31] which he especially addressed to the bishops with whom he had been associated "and as many more as are of their moderation and love of our common peace and concord." It was a noble plea from one who professed himself beyond any relief or help and interested only for his brethren's sake, the sake of the church, and the betterment of his country. "My time of service is near its end." He declared that the English religion had reached a crisis in which Nonconformists could hope for no relief from those in authority, "for they love Rome more than us and desire our bricks without straw. . . . The Nonconformist has always loved and honored the Conformist who preached spiritually and in Christian love. . . . We have had no wish for benefices, or power only to be pastors to the volunteers of the parish. Could there be only a limited toleration we could yet be brought to a happy concord and England to a better reformation than she has ever had and without any hurt to Diocese or Parish."

In the postscript[32] Baxter outlines the Presbyterian purpose as distinctly Puritan: "A Puritan is one that is no more against and as much for bishops, liturgy and ceremonies as in any books I have long since published myself to be." Baxter made clear by his own experiences that persecution was aimed at preaching in itself, not at what was preached, and made an earnest plea to all liberal churchmen for limited toleration.

This later period saw a large number of conformist pamphlets, both clerical and secular, voicing an appeal for toleration.[33] In most of these pamphlets there is recognized a

---

31. Richard Baxter, *An Apology for the Nonconformist Ministry*.

32. The main part seems to have been written in 1668-1669; it was published now in answer to a sermon by Dr. Stillingfleet with the postscript added.

33. See E. Pearce, *The Conformists' Second Plea for the Nonconform-*

clear separation of the Nonconformist from political intrigue and treasonable acts, the spiritual character of Nonconformity, the great need of peace and unity in the church, and the relation of liberty of conscience to the civil liberty of the individual. In some pamphlets is stated the great need of Protestant unity as a defence against growing Catholicism.

There is persistent attention given to unity in order to safeguard economic interests against the loss of wealth and the increasing poverty which was becoming a heavy burden on the parish. Suggestions were made for the employment of the poor, for the establishment of workingmen's schools, for the care of children of the poor, and for instilling temperance and the right rules of conduct. These suggestions were made not only in behalf of the poor but also as a defense of the rich against rebellion and of the country's peace.

Censorship was mainly used to prohibit Nonconformist publications, and in these efforts a certain type of informer was developed who ferreted out the unlawful presses that were engaged in publishing pamphlets which it was clear could not pass the censor. The business of both informer and censor was profitable, for conviction was certain; the fines were large and made sure by the seizure of all properties as well as the persons engaged in publishing, writing, or possessing such unlawful materials.[34]

There were two conformist pamphlets during the period which somewhat disturbed the Puritan group, especially the Presbyterians. These were Stillingfleet's *Mischief of Sep-*

ists; Anon., *Liberty of Conscience in its Order to Universal Peace impartially stated;* J. Humphrey, *Two Steps of a Nonconformist Minister;* J. Corbet, *An Account given of the Principles and Practices of several Nonconformists;* Anon., *The Grounds of Unity in Religion, or an Expedient for a General Conformity and Pacification;* Anon., *A Peaceable Plea for Union and Peace;* J. Jones, *Nonconformity not Inconsistent with Loyalty.*

34. *Calendar of State Papers, Domestic,* 1677-1678, pp. 691-92; 1683, Sept. 6, p. 374. L'Estrange published the *Observator,* 1678-1685, which the Nonconformists charged was paid for by the government to secure evidence against them from publishers.

aration (London, 1681) and a sermon of Tenison, *Giving of Alms,* in the same year. Both men had consistently defended Presbyterian and Congregational Puritanism, and there seemed to be a feeling that their new criticisms were due to the persistent opposition of the High-Church Anglicans to their leniency and also to their desire to keep their Anglican relations clear. Baxter was especially perturbed and felt called upon to restate the position of Nonconformity generally, and his own position particularly. Tenison's sermon laid itself open to pungent criticism, which was quickly forthcoming from both Nonconformists and Anglican laymen. The sarcastic answer came quickly that, according to the complaints of many conformists themselves, in many parishes the only regular attendants at the Anglican services were those who were forced to attend in order legally to receive public charity and that charity was necessary for the Nonconformists only because of their deprivation of property and the fines exacted under the penal laws. But generally the situation was ᵈeemed too serious for such light treatment. On the whole, the pamphlet material from 1678 to 1685 was more judicial than it had formerly been, more serious and less controversial in character, as if recognizing the dangers of Roman influence and the effort of the government to stamp out opposition in both religion and politics.

Through this period the informers were constantly complaining of mistreatment, arrests, fines, and bodily injury, and contempt on the part of officials and their refusal to act on evidence. One can see in the refusal of churchmen to participate in prosecutions, in the attitude of lay conformity, in the constantly increasing strength of Parliament's opposition to the King, in the firmness of Nonconformity itself, and in its readiness to suffer if necessary but to resist by all legal means, that the time was fast approaching when the matter must be settled. Burnet had already prepared to flee to the continent, Bunyan was long since in prison, and

Baxter awaited imprisonment by James.   When James's
Declaration of Indulgence appeared, it was clear that the
real foe of the Anglican church and of the liberty of Englishmen was the Roman church and the High-Churchmen in
their support of the absolute power of the King.

The period of 1675-1685, with the struggles which it
entailed, had not been futile nor were its results all on the
debit side.   The churchmen, especially the Low-Churchmen,
had been increasingly anxious over the indifference and growing disrespect shown to religion.   The acceptance of the
Puritan Sabbath by legal enactment in 1677 was an attempt
to put emphasis upon the controlled life apart from the Sunday service as needed for the good of the religious community.   The bishop's visitation was urged and was taken
with more seriousness.   There was more exhortation to god-
liness and decency in secular life.   Churchmen were more
carefully scrutinized, absenteeism was frowned upon, more
care was taken in the education of candidates for ordination,
and an attempt was made at supervision of those who had
been ordained but were still lacking definite appointment.
In many places the charity schools of the Nonconformists
were studied and copied, and the parish priest, rector or
curate, was put in charge.   The family visitation by the curate
and his regular catechising of the young were urged, and as
far as possible enforced. Many pamphlets were published to
guide and exhort the clergy to better and more faithful work,
and many of the best of these went into innumerable editions, showing clearly a new interest and earnestness of many
of the clergy.

What was true of the conformist clergy was if possible even
more true of the Puritan group. The older generation, they
who had borne the brunt of the long struggle, were fast dis-
appearing, and their places were being taken by a new generation.   Each new survey had shown the presence of new
names and the absence of old ones among the Puritan lead-

ers. The establishment of Nonconformist training schools for
the ministry had been responsible for a new leadership as
dogged as the old one and imbued with the best spiritual
heritage which Puritanism had to offer.   Long suffering
had purged much of the dross of the earlier authoritative
Puritanism from the body, had given more emphasis to its
spiritual growth, and had brought closer unity among the
Protestant sects. Puritanism emphasized the social needs of
the body politic and stood out as a model of Christian life in
its support and succor of its fellows in distress and in its ami-
cable relations with its detractors.   Puritans were criminals
only for liberty of conscience and law breakers only to uphold that individual right which they believed was the
Englishman's heritage.   They were active in the efforts to
purify the social body of its dross; they endeared themselves
to those whom they served and were respected by the Anglican laity as well as by a large part of the clergy.

When Owen died during the severe London persecution,
it was noted that the old rebel had a most popular funeral
with one hundred carriages in attendance.   Calamy, con-
spicuous in all the controversies since 1660, offered a bishopric
by Charles II, a moderate man often in consultation with
Anglicans to find a formula for comprehension, had gone
but had left a son to further his work and to wear his mantle.
Jacomb, one of the most spiritual and best beloved Puritans,
had died in prison deeply mourned, and his memory was
long respected even by his enemies.   Thomas Goudge died,
the Apostle to Wales who had set up three or four hundred
schools, employed teachers, paid the expenses of 2,000 poor
children, printed 8,000 Bibles in Welsh, published and scat-
tered several hundred copies of the *Whole Duty of Man*.
Stillingfleet, Dean of St. Paul's, declared him to have been
the most perfect example of Christ among all mankind. These
were the men, along with Manton, Bunyan, Baxter and
Howe, who had borne the stress of the battle for religious

liberty, and when during James's reign Baxter and Manton were thrown into prison, a large number of the bishops united to offer their aid to nullify the arrests and to extend their sympathy.

The time was fast approaching when the Anglican church must rechart its course or lose the sympathy of its broader-minded leaders and its more intelligent followers. It was fortunate indeed that the saner Puritanism had earned the respect of so large a leadership within the church, and it was also fortunate for the Anglican church that these broader-minded leaders were extending their influence not only among the laymen but were also influencing the policy of the church itself. Thus when the crisis of James's reign came there was full harmony of thought among all the Protestant groups and full support for the church as it assumed a leadership in the struggle for liberty, religious, civil, and constitutional, against a dynasty that persistently refused to permit a limit to be set to its power and authority.

Above all, this later period, with its growing fear of Catholicism, its strong opposition to Charles's economic measures and his flouting of the later parliaments, had brought together again the Puritans in religion and the constitutionalists who feared the growth of that divine right which the high Anglicans had done so much to encourage and the King so much to establish. It was already clear by 1685 that England must face again the struggle undertaken under Charles I. Through the long reign of Charles II, Puritans had upheld the principle of liberty in religion in the face of almost continual persecution. They could well afford to allow the leadership in this new struggle to pass to secular hands, since that leadership must be their support if it won against James. The great value of their consistent suffering is seen in the general support given them down to the coming of William and Mary, and the very general recognition of the oneness of the struggle.

V

PURITANISM

IN THE REVOLUTION

OF 1688

CHARLES II died on February 6th, 1685. One can almost hear the sigh of relief which came from Nonconformity in spite of the belief that it must fare worse under the new King. Charles had associated Nonconformity with the Whig party, which he knew he must destroy if he were to attain his end. He had promised relief, tried an indulgence, and spent the last years of his life in the determined effort to destroy the Nonconformists. The High-Churchmen had gone even farther, for as Baxter charged, many of them seemed ready "to travel the road back to Rome." There was much discussion of the older Laudian principles of the King's divine right, nonresistance and passive obedience. Many High-Churchmen admitted that Anglicanism in its point of view differed less from Roman than from Nonconformist principles, since Rome laid emphasis upon the divine character of the church and the king. Certainly there was little hope or light ahead for the long-suffering Nonconformist. Yet the Nonconformist was for the moment relieved, though he must have dreaded the change, for with Catholicism he could not compromise.

England received James well. He had declared himself ready to uphold the church "as by law established" and his frankness in refusing the church service and the setting up of his own Catholic chapel seemed a good omen, for it suggested that he was at least honest. The failure of the Monmouth rebellion was in reality a token of the nation's acceptance of James. The outrageous work of Jeffreys in settling affairs with Monmouth's supporters should have given people pause, but they were satisfied for the time to put the blame on the agent. James took quick action. His first parliament, whose election he had supervised under Charles's measures, was as blind as the Anglican church. He repeated his declaration regarding the established church, and it was satisfied. Indeed, the committee of the whole House prepared a resolution asking the King to enforce the laws against all dissenters from the Church of England but laid it aside on the request of the ministry, who probably saw in it some embarrassment for the King. Parliament went on to grant funds for the support of an army altogether out of proportion to the danger of Monmouth's futile efforts. Before its prorogation it had put into James's hands the financial means to go forward from the point where Charles left off and had added an armed force to carry out the King's will.[1] He had only to come to terms with Louis of France and to get his army disciplined and under control, and the way to success was achieved.

Fortunately James was both reckless and impatient. He had not the keenness or experience of Charles, neither Charles's intelligence nor his understanding of the English mind. His forthrightness, which his friends called honesty, was merely lack of judgment and good sense, and his obstinacy only made clear his utter lack of statesmanship. Burnet, whom the King as prince had refused to see, was the first but not the last to go to the Continent, there to watch the course of events until his return with William.[2] Baxter was brought to trial before Jeffreys' court, roundly abused and sentenced to jail pending the payment of five hundred

1. Burnet, *History of his own Time*, III, 6-7.   2. *Ibid.*, II, 2-4.

marks, an impossible sum, and spent two quiet years in prison until the indulgence released him after surety had been furnished for his good behavior.[3]

The activity against Protestant Nonconformity was not lessened during the early part of the reign, and unfortunately the church continued its support of the work. The Argyle revolt as well as the attempt of Monmouth gave a basis for the government's activity if not for its methods, and the hunting out of those "infected" became a sport. To Jeffreys it made no difference as to the charge and very little as to the evidence. Those who fell into his hands found no escape though like Lady Lisle they had been innocent of any thought of rebellion. Even when no further remnant of the rebel group was left, the work went on and a new batch of informers took up the hunt. The wealthy Nonconformist was mulcted into furnishing blackmail or paying heavy fines. The jails were filled again to overflowing. The Quakers petitioned the King for mercy, declaring that fifteen hundred Quakers had gone to prison in the first year and a half of James's reign.[4] Jeremy White had collected a list of 60,000 Nonconformists who had suffered since 1660. An offer from James of £1,000 for the list was refused by White.[5] Until April, 1687, because of Monmouth's Rebellion, the Nonconformists suffered the severest persecution through which they had been called to pass, largely under the charge of rebellion; yet they had remained steadfast. It is little wonder that they drew a long breath of relief when the indulgence was issued or that many were moved to present addresses of thankfulness to the King. They had languished or died in prison, had been sold as slaves to the Barbados, had emigrated to the Continent, had suffered financial ruin, and had

3. Calamy, *Nonconformist's Memorial*, I, 240; Clark, *History of English Nonconformity*, II, 105.

4. Neal, *History of the Puritans*, II, 319, 321-22; Sir James Mackintosh, *History of the Revolution*, p. 150.

5. Clark, *op. cit.*, II, 162, note; Neal, *op. cit.*, II, 322.

left their families in poverty. Yet so far as one can discover, they had kept the faith, and their numbers were little diminished. Many Anglicans left their church, disgusted with its acquiescence in or aid to the inhuman efforts of the government, while moderate churchmen became active in their protest against the church's support of James's designs.

By 1686 the courts had recognized the King's dispensing power. He at once began to appoint unfit timeservers to offices in the church and to encourage churchmen to declare their adherence to Rome without resigning office. The controversy over Sharp, rector of St. Giles, who had preached a strong sermon against the encroachment of the Roman Catholics, forced the church to see the issue more clearly. Compton, Bishop of London, was told to dismiss Sharp, and upon his asserting that he could but act as judge if the case were brought to him, James reëstablished the old ecclesiastical commission that had been dissolved by the Long Parliament; it suspended Compton from his office.[6] This incident brought some high Anglicans to their senses and the church's protest that such action was unlawful was without avail. James had taken the bit in his teeth and meant to ride the church down as he had the rebels and the Nonconformists. By 1687 James's purpose had become clear to the nation. His ministry was reorganized to make sure of its support of his plans. Some of the nobility declared for the Roman Catholic church, High-Churchmen stood aside, and much discussion was given to presenting and comparing Roman doctrines and liturgy with those of England. Archbishop Sancroft, appointed on the High Commission, instead of protesting absented himself on the plea of illness;[7] James could well believe that he could command the church. The Low-Churchmen and the Nonconformists he could not command. The latter, long protestants against the formalized

6. Burnet, *op. cit.*, III, 106-7.
7. *Victoria County History of London*, I, 345-46.

religion of the Stuarts, were the first to warn of the danger.
Most of them, because of their suspicion of its purpose, had
refused to respond to the pressure that they present addresses
to the King for the indulgence. In the short period of two
years preceding the Revolution, more anti-Catholic pamphlets
appeared despite strict censorship than had appeared through
the long reign of Charles II. The moderate churchman
had joined the Nonconformist in protest. To the student of
freedom of thought in religion the pamphlets carry a new
interest. Much emphasis is put upon the intent of the laws
placed on the statute books under Charles II. It was declared that they were meant not to persecute religion but to
attack rebellion that paraded under religious disguise.[8] Anglicans had not emphasized this point of view before nor listened
to such protests from the Nonconformist. Now Anglicans
protested that the Nonconformists had shown themselves the
most spiritual group within the kingdom and should be
brought back, not by persecution but by an emphasis upon the
spiritual character of the church, which had forgotten its real
purpose while acting as prosecutor for the state against rebellion. There is a very general appeal for toleration as the
means of unity, especially stressed in the fact of the present
danger of the Catholic development.[9] Under James the
Presbyterian Puritan was strongly in favor of toleration, and
seemed to have forgotten comprehension in the face of the
danger, although both within and without the church voices
were still raised for the comprehension of the conservative-
minded among Nonconformists. Before the end of 1686
even the High-Churchmen had recognized the need of culti-
vating the older enemy, and instructions were issued by Archbishop Sancroft for the better treatment of Nonconformists.[10]

8. Anon., *The New Test of the Church of England's Loyalty;* William
Darrell, *The Layman's Opinion.*

9. Anon., *A Letter from a Gentleman in the Country to Friends in
London* (1687).

10. Cardwell, *Documentary Annals,* II, 302; *A Second Collection of
Papers Relating to the Present Juncture of Affairs in England.*

It is unnecessary to recount the steps taken by James which brought the nation with the High-Churchmen to revive the cry, "The church is in danger." The important aspect of the period is its near approach to conditions of the rebellion of 1640. Certainly the Nonconformists, even with the support of the Low-Churchmen, could hardly have challenged James's power in 1688 any more than they had been able to challenge Charles's in 1639. With James II, as with Charles I, the issue was that of the arbitrary power of the King in civil and religious affairs, but fortunately for English unity James II had added the issue of Anglicanism against Roman Catholicism. Charles I had kept close to the High Church, and the Long Parliament for a time drew to itself those who saw the real issue, the liberty of the individual, in all its aspects, as did the nation in 1688. However, this group was repelled by the further demands after Charles had accepted the legislation of 1640-1642 and the rebels found themselves a small minority whose power was upheld only by an army. James II set the whole nation against him by alienating the Anglican church. There was no question of the nation's allegiance to the church, though James did not believe it. When it became aware of its own danger and the larger aspects of liberty, the church easily carried the nation with it, and this support made the difference in the two movements. This point has had little emphasis from historians, who have usually laid the greatest stress upon the constitutional and economic aspects of the Revolution.

The Revolution of 1688 was successful because with "the church in danger" the nation rallied to its support and the general fear of Catholicism effected unanimity. It is certainly true that the economic aspects of the Revolution were more important in 1688 than in 1640, not so much because of the King's hostility as because of his preference for the Catholic countries on the Continent. The constitutional aspect was more important in 1640 because of the King's youth and

the strong position of the dynasty. Until the birth of James's
son the constitutionalists were inclined to wait for James II
to die to restore the balance of power between King and
Parliament, but the Church of England could not wait. Certainly the High-Church party did not grasp the great issue
of the Revolution, the liberty of the individual in its religious
aspect, nor, for that matter, in its other aspects, but they did
see the danger of their own overthrow. Against James II
the nation was for a moment united. His purpose had become clear. The nation would have nothing of the Roman
control and were prepared to challenge the King on this
issue. Fortunately the Catholic issue had made clear to all
groups the King's purpose to put behind him as well all the
rights and liberties of Englishmen. As one reads over the
charges against the Stuarts in the Declaration of Right, it
becomes clear that the contention of the Nonconformists for
liberty in religion had again broadened to a program of
liberty in constitutional and civil as well as religious matters.
This view puts additional emphasis upon the religious-mind-
edness of the seventeenth century and on the part this spirit
played in the Revolution of 1688, and emphasizes greatly the
importance of the Puritan contributions to this later Stuart
period.[11] For out of this struggle for liberty of worship
comes quickly thereafter the expansion of the idea that liberty
is the Englishman's heritage and that to secure it, the idea
of the divine character of the dynasty must be thrust aside. It
was fortunate, too, that the established church was able to
see its own danger from James and had no time to question
the further issues that the Revolution must face. It was also
fortunate that the movement for comprehension had grown.
The elections for the Convention Parliament temporarily
swept into power those who sympathized with the Low
Church and Nonconformity. The Declaration of Right put
these issues with those of civil and constitutional liberty to

11. T. Lathbury, *History of the Non-Jurors,* pp. 55-56.

the fore and insisted that their security demanded the recognition of a king who would accept them and who was able to protect them. The decision of the four hundred Nonjurors to withdraw from the church rather than accept this conclusion emphasizes the gravity of the problem and the confusion in the minds of the Anglicans who could participate in James's overthrow but could not face its consequences.

John Locke, who had retired to Holland when James became king, published the first clear statement of the philosophy of the Revolution before William had crossed the channel.[12] Republished in England, it with three more letters on toleration defending Nonconformists, broadened religious freedom into the rights of the individual in all aspects as against arbitrary government, accepted the sovereignty of the people, and dismissed the doctrine of the divine right of kings and bishops as an illusion. To his mind, the right of revolution must be called into play when a king betrayed his people. Locke had no objection to a state church, but he clearly saw the possibility of such a church sacrificing the fundamental rights of the people unless checked, and his answer was full toleration in religion.

Fortunately the Restoration period had seen a steadily growing change within the church. The moderate churchmen were first dismayed at the severe treatment of Nonconformists, then refused to participate in such activity and slowly repudiated the High-Church doctrines of nonresistance, passive obedience, and divine right. In this change the more intelligent laity had acquiesced; hence, when the high Anglicans refused the oath and withdrew, the church was able to replace them with reasoned Low-Churchmen and to maintain its position with the laity. This is not to say that they wanted comprehension. William's hasty action in naming a number of Nonconformist bishops probably awakened a new fear on the part of the church and certainly stiffened its resistance to

12. John Locke, *A Letter concerning Toleration.*

his expressed desire for comprehension and for revision of the liturgy and the Book of Common Prayer.[13]

The coming of William to England and his acceptance by the English with Mary, his wife, as king and queen was a severe test of the high Anglican church. In a letter to his diocese written in July, 1689, after the trial of the seven bishops, Sancroft stressed the spiritual character of the dissenters and asked the churchmen to treat them with special leniency. This letter was praised as the voice of the church by Wake, Bishop of Lincoln, who recommended its acceptance as such by the entire church body. Bishop Wake felt it to have been a great mistake that a compromise had not been accepted in 1660.[14] Many churchmen who had been silent through the earlier period now made their voices heard in

13. The clearest statement of the position and attitude of the high Anglican is found in a pamphlet by Charles Leslie (*Querela Temporum, or the Danger of the Church of England*). He writes: "I am assured that much the greatest part of the clergy have come into government as you and I have done, out of a prospect to preserve the church. For if all had stuck out we did dreadfully apprehend that the Presbyterian church, considering our King's education and bias that way and their great merit in the revolution and our reluctance which we could not conceal (and at first many of us did not desire to conceal it as the nation clearly saw), . . . would have been set up or something like it [and the whole church overturned]. We were not sure William did not see our reluctance and bide his time to overthrow us [since the laity had little zeal for the church]. The tide runs fast toward a fanatical level both in Church and State. . . . The people are against us in inclination and in Parliament. . . . You see our dilemma, for if we stick to passive obedience in the high sense we must condemn what we have done and continue to do. But if we call that an error then we own our church had been all along a false guide and that dissenters have taught the truth. So the church of England has been forced to shift its position from passive obedience, non-resistance, and divine right and accept a new oath over their old one. The wretched deference for this apostacy makes matters worse [when] taking the oath to King William they reserve a right to King James as everyone knows and with the loss of prestige to themselves

'When all the argument is out
'Tis interest resolves the doubt.' "

14. Cardwell, *op. cit.*, II, 372. This was emphasized by many pamphlets of the time (cf. Anon., *A Letter to a Gentleman in Brussels containing an Account of the People's Revolt from the Crown; W. D., The Present Interest in Matters of Religion Stated*).

favor of a more lenient treatment, and for the moment the persecuting group were silenced.[15]

But when the Convention Parliament was called and the question of the kingship was opened in Parliament, this silence passed and the High-Churchmen saw the dilemma clearly. A petition to William asked that the birth of the Prince should be definitely and finally adjudged since they could accept James's flight as abdication and Mary as queen if the Prince was adjudged to be not a true son of James.[16] The High-Churchmen led the fight in Parliament to act on this theory and to make Mary queen and recognize William only as the Queen's husband. If they now gave up the theories of divine right, of non-resistance and passive obedience, they were really accepting as a fact that the church had been wrong since 1660 and that the dissenters had been right, and they felt they could not face such admission with its resulting effects upon the established church.[17] They lost the fight because the layman in Parliament at the moment was more interested in civil and religious liberty than in High-Church theory. There seemed nothing to do but, when the occasion arose, to refuse the oath and give up office when and if the refusal necessitated such a measure.[18] As a result the most conservative High-Churchmen became dissenters and the Low-Churchmen who had made no point of the High-Church theories were given the places of church leadership. William appointed twenty Presbyterians to church office, and vacancies made by resignations were filled with Low-Churchmen. Tillotson, whose Puritan background

15. Cf. note 21, below.
16. "A Memorial of the Protestants of England to the Prince and Princess of Orange," *A Collection of Papers relating to the Present Juncture,* no. 14.
17. Anon., *The New Test of the Church of England's Loyalty.*
18. Anon., *The Examination of the Case of the suspended Bishops in Answer to the Apology for them;* George D'Oyly, *Life of Sancroft,* appendix; Francis Fullwood, *Obedience due to the present King;* Anon., *A Modest Examination of the new Oath of Allegiance.*

was strong and whose liberal ideas were well known, was made Archbishop of Canterbury, Burnet was appointed to the bishopric of Salisbury, and the church was saved from the worst effects of the virtual reversal of its theories.[19] Many of the lesser churchmen who maintained their adherence to High Church took the oath with reluctance in order to keep their places. Largely through their suffrage in Convocation the efforts toward comprehension at this time failed, though the spirit of the principles upon which comprehension was based was maintained within the church and became the basis of the eighteenth-century evangelicalism under the influence of the spiritual teaching of William Law and John Wesley.

The passage of the Toleration Act was the immediate answer of the English laity and Parliament to the religious question. Such an act was recognized as necessary even if comprehension, which Parliament refused, should be accepted by the Convocation. There was considerable discussion of the problem in the interval, and Archbishop Tillotson seems to have been convinced that comprehension would not be refused. Burnet addressed a pamphlet[20] to Convocation in which the case was finely and broadly stated, and a petition and counsel were sent from "many Divines and others" to Convocation when it was in session.[21] Archbishop Tillotson advised William to establish a commission of bishops to prepare matters for Convocation and he himself drew up a program entitled "Concessions which will probably be made by the Church of England for the Union of Protestants."[22] In this program ministers would be asked to subscribe to but

19. The general acceptance of the Church of England after William's new appointments probably saved the Anglican church (see note 13, above). William appointed Low-Churchmen to the vacant places mainly, but included a number of Presbyterians.

20. Gilbert Burnet, *The Case of Compulsion in Matters of Religion stated.*

21. *To the Right Reverend and Reverend Bishops and Clergy . . . in Convocation. . . . The Humble Petition of Many Divines. . . .*

22. Thomas Birch, *Life of Tillotson*, p. 182.

one general declaration: "That we do submit to the doctrine, discipline and worship of the Church of England as it shall be established by law and promise to teach and practice accordingly." He proposed to remove from the liturgy all grounds of exception to make the ceremonies "indifferent," to require no additional ordination for those who had been ordained, to revise the canons, especially those regarding the reformation of manners, and to regulate and reform the ecclesiastical courts.

The commission was appointed, but its members disagreed on almost the whole program, those opposed mostly refusing to attend the sessions of the commission, and Tillotson advised that Convocation be permitted to settle the matter.[23] He as archbishop had expected to be made prolocutor of the lower house and believed he could persuade and guide the discussions to accomplish the purpose. In this he was mistaken, for the house at once showed its opposition to any plan of comprehension by electing Dr. William Jane of Oxford, a high and strict Anglican, as prolocutor. After a long period of discussion and wrangling, the whole program of change was discarded, and William, in disgust, dissolved the assembly and refused to recall it until 1701. Tillotson was, however, firm in trying to reform the church from within, and the bishops accepted and acted upon his charges to them. He was liberal even with the Nonjurors who wished to attend services but refused to join in the prayers for the King. His thesis was that it was no use to require prayer from those whose hearts were not in their prayers and that attempts to force uniformity were unchristian and futile. He, at least, went far to help the church recover from the falseness of its position and to center attention upon the simple program of Christian living, thus promoting the reformation

23. Dr. William Jane, leader of the opposition to Tillotson's program, had certainly salved his conscience when he took the oath to William. His bitter opposition to Tillotson probably was to show a repentance for his oath. Like many others, he defended himself by "saving the church."

which was so greatly needed after the turmoil and dissolute-
ness of the Stuart period.   The King and the Queen gave
him their confidence and accepted his advice, and he was able
to give a new and potent character to the leadership of the
church which was greatly aided by the absence of Convocation
and of any authority to question his procedure.[24]

The work of easing the position of Nonconformity made
little progress after the passing of the Toleration Act.[25]
This measure withdrew three of the four acts known as the
Clarendon Code.   The Corporation Act together with the
Test Act was left to plague Nonconformity through the
coming century.   The Act of Toleration set free all who were
under the penalties of the former laws either by fine or imprisonment.   However, it required all meetings to be held
with open doors and the meeting places to be registered.
Ministers and teachers were exempted from holding civil
office, and laymen holding such offices and refusing the oath
must act by deputy.   Papists and Unitarians were excepted
from the benefits of the law.   All efforts to withdraw the
Test and Corporation Acts failed in Parliament, and Nonconformists were left compromised as to the rights of citizenship.   They were now put in a false position over which for
the next few years there was much discussion.   The Nonconformist laymen continued to hold office by subscribing to the
oath and attending the church communion once within the
year in which they were elected; or they refused this and
acted by deputy.   They were not in their own opinion too
greatly compromised by this, since from 1660 onward Puritan dissenters had maintained this right and had practiced
such attendance in addition to, or in the absence of, their
own services.

The conditions of society under the Protestant religion in
1689 have always been under controversy.   The church has

24. Birch, op. cit., pp. 335 ff.; Edmund Calamy, An Historical Account
of my own Life, I, 210, 212.   25. Pickering, Statutes, IX, 19.

been eulogized as being in a most flourishing and promising condition, marred only by the divisions which the laws had permitted. On the other hand, there has been a tendency to regard society in general as in a deplorable state in which all the virtues had disappeared and the vices prospered.[26] As a matter of fact, there is little reason to accept either of the extreme views. As one reviews the writings of the seventeenth century he is struck with the vehemence of utterance from 1640 onwards as to the godlessness of English social life. Puritans had a tendency so to describe the conditions which they found and readily ascribed them to the influence of the church under James I and Charles I. The restored Anglicans of 1660 likewise charged to the Puritanism of the Commonwealth the prevalence of the same evils.

The seventeenth century was one in which there was a great lack of the niceties of life. The ethics and morality of a later age make it difficult to evaluate conditions unless one is familiar with the preceding era as well as with the habits of pamphleteers. When the Puritan wished to explain the abolition of old customs he put the emphasis upon their abuses. The May Day festival was held responsible for the "loss of the virtue of the majority of the participants." The Sunday regulations of the early Stuarts were supposed to have led "to drunkenness, swearing and all sorts of evils." This is, of course, true in a sense, but no attempt was made to distinguish between causes. Virtue was not essentially a religious matter in old England. Nor for that matter, were drunkenness and swearing. It was, in truth, the Puritan who first put emphasis upon the relation of religion to life; and one of the best criteria for the growing Puritan influence is seen in the attention given to this application during and after

26. [William III], *Directions to our Archbishop and Bishops for the Preserving of Unity in the Church and Purity of the Christian Faith;* Francis Atterbury, *A Representation of the present State of Religion,* a report drawn up in 1711 for the lower house of Convocation; Cardwell, *op. cit.,* II, 330-33.

the Restoration. Generally speaking, the public debauchery
during the reign of Charles II was confined to a comparatively narrow circle, and Parliament in harmony with the Puritan desire for reformatiọn early began legislation on Sunday
observance and against drunkenness and swearing.

One great weakness of the Anglican Restoration in 1660 is
found in the necessity of placing so many men unfit in morals
and intelligence into the places left vacant by the forced
withdrawal of the Nonconformists. Unfortunately the church
could not recover from the effects of this in the short period
of Stuart rule. There was under the circumstances a necessity for pluralism and for absenteeism that the period found
it impossible to remedy. It made the laws passed for the
regulation of conduct difficult to enforce, and in some places
and at particular times it nullified them. But as 1689 ap-
proaches, there is little difference between conformist and
Nonconformist pamphlets regarding this problem. To be
sure a good many churchmen, feeling that they were on the
defensive, placed responsibility on the Nonconformists as far
as possible, and the necessity of the secret religious assembly
gave opportunity for such a charge. But among the saner
leaders on both sides these conditions were deplored and
efforts were ceaselessly made to remedy them. This can
best be seen in the continued directions given to parish priests
to visit and catechise, which were made by bishops in their
visitations and instructions and as well in those of the arch-
bishops to the diocesans. Neither is it to be wondered at that
the century gave much emphasis to human as against Christian
actions. The policy of enforcing a particular kind of religion,
whether Anglican or Puritan, the savagery engendered by the
nature of the civil war, the indifference to morals and ethics
in high places, made the efforts of Anglican and Puritan
largely futile so long as the church gave so much of its time
and attention to enforcement of laws against Nonconformists

rather than to the cultivation of the Christian life and spirit among the parishioners.

The question of 1689 really was, would the Toleration Act bring this additional dividend as well as give the right of liberty in religion to the Nonconformist. That it did much to remedy the situation is undoubted. But unfortunately laws could not change men's nature. A half century of religious hatred could not be eliminated swiftly by either one or both of the groups. The Nonconformist continued to find himself face to face with bitter hostility and hatred even when the law fairly protected him, and his own influence was distinctly marred by his belief in the too often expressed contempt for the Anglican church. The comprehension desired by Tillotson and Baxter along with toleration would have had a far better effect upon the religious life of England. It would have brought the larger group of Nonconformists into the state church, would have changed but little the ritual, forms and ceremonies, would soon have eliminated the influence of the unconfirmed leadership[27] and would have given united efforts for the application of religious principles to the life of the people. Had this been done the Toleration Act would have put an end in very large part to the long struggle between Puritanism and Anglicanism and would more completely have separated religion and politics in the England of the future.

27. Tillotson's program provided that all new bishops must be confirmed in the Anglican church so that within the generation a real unity would have been secured.

VI

TOLERATION

UNDER WILLIAM & MARY

AND ANNE

Like all revolutions, the Revolution of 1688 had a clear notion of what was not wanted but a much less clear idea of what should be its positive character. There was unity in the hostility to Roman Catholicism which was largely responsible for James's overthrow. With James in France and with William's Dutch army in control, unity vanished. The call for a convention parliament came before the new issues were clear. So, as far as possible for the period, the Parliament was free from the religious antagonism so prevalent at the time. As the debates went forward, the House of Lords, always conservative, perhaps because of the presence of the bishops, saw more clearly than the lower house the meaning of the things which they found necessary to do. Thus it was the Lords who fought to make William regent and to make Mary queen, or at least to force some declaration as to the illegitimacy of the Prince definite enough to rid themselves of the old dynasty.

The lower house were the revolutionists. They wanted the throne vacated. They drew up the Declaration of Right preparatory to settling the throne anew. They discarded James and his son without bothering to decide whether the son were legitimate or not. They, no doubt, would have made Mary queen with William as consort if that had been possible, but they readily accepted both as rulers because it was necessary. The Bill of Rights was their peculiar gift.[1] They put into it all the grievances which the nation had suffered under the later Stuarts and declared the arbitrary authority of the king illegal.[2] They renewed the declaration of 1660 that the government of England should be by King, Lords and Commons, but they reversed the order and by their action put the Commons as standing for the nation first.

So far the Commons were quite positive as to their course. They were equally positive that religious persecution should cease and that the church should be definitely subordinated to the secular power by revising the oath of office for all who helped to govern in state or church.[3] As to discussing or settling the established church, they quickly turned that matter over to Convocation, whose members, recognizing that comprehension was a church matter, knew the difficulties in the way. At this point the Anglican church prepared to fight the issue. Some of the peculiar beliefs of the High Church had gone with the Revolution, and unless its proponents rallied, the whole structure of the church would be changed. The oath of allegiance to William and Mary had been required and some eight bishops with nearly four hundred lesser churchmen had found it necessary to refuse the oath.[4] They must be faithful to the old oath to James, or give up the High-Church theory of the divine right of the king and

1. *Revised Statutes,* II, 9.

2. The Bill of Rights was the Covenant's justification for the overthrow of the Stuart dynasty; it was therefore a document of grievances as well as a declaration of rights of the nation against the King.

3. Pickering, *Statutes,* IX, 8.

4. The nonjuring group included three of the bishops and the archbishop, all of whom were tried for refusing to read the second indulgence of James II. Under William and Mary a period of five months was allowed in which to take the oath. A number of pamphlets appeared defending the oath. Cf. Anon., *A Friendly Conference concerning the New Oath by a Church of England Divine.*

passive obedience on the part of the subject to the ruler. The churchmen were unprepared for the revolution which had taken place. Beyond the destruction of Romanism they had not realized its implications. Now they resolved to make no concessions to the Nonconformists and left the questions regarding the dynasty unanswered for the time because they must. The year 1689 would seem to most historians the end of the period of religious persecution. The Toleration Act was passed by Parliament. The King and Queen were sympathetic with Nonconformity. The Scots were allowed to reëstablish their Presbyterian church, thus placing the Anglicans among the Nonconformists in Scotland. In England, however, Parliament was unprepared to go beyond the Toleration Act. The attempt to withdraw the Test and Corporation Acts failed. Though the Nonconformist might be tolerated he was not to be put on a parity with members of the state church. Enough of the old laws were to be retained to keep him in his place.

The lower house of Convocation had followed the lower house of Parliament in refusing guidance from the upper house of bishops. Instead of choosing the archbishop to preside, it selected the High-Churchman who had led the revolt in a committee appointed by William to draw up changes which the Convocation, it was hoped, would adopt. Dr. William Jane from the Cambridge faculty had taken the oath required by Parliament, but he was an uncompromising High-Churchman who remained within the church to aid in holding it true to its course.[5] His selection as chairman made any changes impossible, and the lower house made it clear that the Anglican church was wholly unprepared, as it always had been, to make any terms with Nonconformity.[6]

5. Many lords both lay and ecclesiastical took the oath for this reason or in order to secure their property; see Burnet, *History of his own Time*, IV, 302-3.

6. Calamy asserted that Nonconformity would have lost two thirds of its followers had the advice of this commission been followed (see his *Historical Account of my own Life*, p. 448). Burnet thought the same.

It must bide its time because the new rulers had put the leadership of the church in Low-Church hands. Hence when on the advice of Archbishop Tillotson, William called Convocation, the lower house refused to make changes or to listen to any advice from the upper house, and William, seeing the mood, prorogued the body and left it in abeyance for ten years.

As to their future course the Anglicans were undecided, possibly because of William's early dismissal of Convocation. They did not trust William in spite of his oath to support the church. His early appointments to fill the Nonjurors' vacant places were from among the Low-Churchmen whom they did not respect. The settlement in Scotland establishing the Presbyterian church seemed ominous, and many churchmen besides Dr. Jane had taken the oath to William and Mary with reserve as necessary to hold office, and perhaps to defend the church against the new government.[7]

This was the situation facing the revolutionary government. William and Mary gave much attention to church reform. William did not attempt to hide his disappointment at the attitude of the High-Churchmen but accepted the situation so far as he felt it necessary. His appointments were from the Low-Churchmen or men of moderate views, and he probably hoped to find a change of sentiment in time. He was sensible that reform was needed aside from any questions at issue, and to this he turned his attentions. He early instructed Archbishop Tillotson to urge upon the clergy more attention to the laity in the parish, more catechising and preaching, and especially more regular observance of the sacraments, as well as more careful attention to social evils.

7. In the pamphlets on this subject the independence of the church from the state was asserted, hence the oath to the King unnecessary. See Henry Dodwell, *The Doctrine of the Church of England concerning the Independency of the Clergy on Lay Power;* Anon., *A Letter to a Dissenting Clergyman of the Church of England concerning the Oath of Allegiance and Obedience to the Present Government.*

He urged less absenteeism, fewer pluralities[8] and greater care
in the matter of ordination.[9]   Mary received more sympathy
from the churchmen as she more nearly represented the old
dynasty, and while she lived William was content to allow
her a free hand in appointments and supervision of church
affairs.   On her death he appointed a clerical commission to
recommend men for church vacancies, whose advice he faithfully followed.[10]

William's carefulness had, however, little effect upon the
High-Churchmen.   Almost at once they turned attention to
means of bringing back James, and the intrigues of the early
years were found to have the active support of all too many
churchmen while it was seen that the greater part of those
who were high Anglican gave their sympathy to such
efforts.[11]   As the reign advanced, the position hardened, and
when it became less possible for political intrigue, attention
was turned against the Nonconformists.   After Convocation
failed to make the desired changes in the service, there was
some hope especially among the Low-Churchmen, that at
least the Presbyterian Puritans would come over to their side,
and this hope, based on the very complacent attitude of the
Presbyterian group, was strengthened when the new meeting houses were registered in so general a way as to be
easily changed into Anglican churches if the opportunity
seemed to warrant it.   The group of Low-Churchmen formed
a society to preach and write in an attempt to persuade such
a move, and some Nonconformists, both clergy and laity, tired
of the long struggles, did go over.   However, charges were
soon made that Nonconformity was growing[12] and, as in the

8. Cardwell, *op. cit.*, II, 384; *Calendar of State Papers, Domestic*, 1689,
pp. 242-43.

9. Norman Sykes, *Church and State in England in the Eighteenth Century*, p. 37.

10. Joseph Addison, *Works*, III, 212.

11. Burnet, *History of his own Time*, IV, 142 ff.

12. Calamy, *Historical Account of my own Life*, p. 449.

past, pamphlets appeared condemning it.[13]   So antagonistic
was the attitude that Baxter was drawn from his seclusion
to pen one of his most effective pamphlets in defense of the
Nonconformist position, tracing it from the Presbyterian support to the Restoration in 1660.[14]   Toward the end of the
reign, attention was called to the prevalence of occasional conformity as practiced by the Presbyterian group and sometimes
by the Independents.[15]   By 1702 the High-Churchmen, encouraged by the fact that Anne sympathized with them in
spite of the Tory Act of Succession of 1701, had become ob-
sessed with the idea of the destruction of the Nonconformists
and the return of the old dynasty, especially now that since
James was dead, the Prince might accept the religion of
Protestant England and the High Church might come into
its own.

Nonconformity was fairly at ease when the Toleration
Act had passed.   Many saw in the failure of comprehension a
strengthening of Nonconformity.   Even many of the Low-
Churchmen felt that perhaps Nonconformity would gain by
that failure, and its strengthening would be a good influence
on the church.   The period from 1689 to 1715 marked an
era of growth in the numbers of dissenters, in their organization, and in their confidence.   The Act of Toleration gave
opportunity for open and public worship, and throughout
the reign meeting houses grew in number. Funds were found
from the faithful.   Wealthy members donated houses or furnished money to build them.   Many of the aristocracy sympathized with the work even when they were not a part of

13. Anon., *An Earnest and Compassionate Suit for Forbearance to the
Learned Writers of some Controversies at Present*; Defoe, *A New Dis-
covery of an Old Intrigue*; Increase Mather, *A Letter of Advice to the
Churches of the Nonconformists in the English Nation.*
    14. Richard Baxter, *English Nonconformity as under Charles II and
James II.*
    15. Burnet, *History of his own Time*, V, 17 ff., 49; Clark, *History of
English Nonconformity*, II, 140 ff.

it, and gave freely.[16] The houses were either permanent meeting houses or private houses licensed for the purpose. It is probable that between 2,000 and 2,400 houses, both permanent and temporary, were licensed through the reign, though many statements gave from 1,000 to 2,500.[17] As had been the case throughout the Stuart period, many of the more timid who had remained in the fold of the church, now that Nonconformity was legalized, came out openly for their Nonconformist belief. The government's attempt at a count made by the church in 1689 put the numbers at 4.5 per cent of the population, or about 250,000. This, as usual, included only those over sixteen years of age, so was not only conservative, as always, but also failed to represent the real situation. By the end of William's reign there was little doubt of the increase. Defoe put the numbers at two million, a mere guess and a palpable exaggeration, but, after all, numbers were never of great importance except as giving heart to the timid.

After 1662 the Nonconformists had been barred from the universities and from church schools. They were therefore very early faced with the problem of education, not only for their ministry, their primary concern, but also for the laity. Driven from the pulpits in 1662, many Oxford- and Cambridge-trained scholars established private schools and gave themselves up to teaching as a means of support. Soon the importance of these schools for the training of ministers became evident since, the Nonconformists having decided after the Conventicle Act to defy the laws, they needed above all an educated clergy. The schools flourished. When closed, the one-man school could easily be established in a new place, and often the schools were supported and protected by the laity who, even though Anglicans, found in them an oppor-

16. H. S. Skeats and C. S. Miall, *History of the Free Churches of England*, p. 157.
17. H. McLachlan, *English Education under the Test Act*, pp. 6 ff.

tunity for education for which they could not afford to pay the universities.

The reign of William and Mary gave great impetus to these schools. Funds from various sources were quickly found to increase the numbers of schools and to give them better equipment. The Presbyterian Fund, a common fund for both Congregational and Presbyterian use, and after the dissolution of the union of the two in 1695 the Congregational Fund of 1695, were but a few of the means for founding and maintaining schools. By 1702 there were forty-seven[18] Nonconformist academies, many of which had opened their doors to both lay and clerical applicants. Moreover their character had improved with increased facilities and many Anglican clergymen were content to send their children to these schools. When Archbishop Sharp complained in the House of Lords of these Nonconformist schools, Lord Wharton could counter his arguments by the simple statement that Sharp's two sons had been educated in one of them, and Bishop Burnet could twit Bishop Compton on the same issue. Thus by 1702 the Nonconformist sects were in the main well organized and in a thriving condition. Undoubtedly their prosperity was a strong reason for the High-Church attempt under Anne to overthrow them. The Anglicans had suffered by the Toleration Act in that the parishioners could no longer be forced to attend church service, and the complaints over empty churches charged the fault to Nonconformity rather than to the real causes.[19] Party hostility, too, by 1702 had become pronounced. Anne was known to be a Tory and a high Anglican, which gave the Anglicans hope that the Nonconformist could be brought to terms and that the influence of the Whig party could be undermined.

There was, as one would suspect, a lack of understanding of the nature of the Revolution and the effect the Act of

18. *Ibid.*, pp. 23, 24.
19. These charges were made by both conformist and Nonconformist for different purposes.

Toleration would have upon the population as a whole. For a long time the church had complained of laxity in church attendance and the Nonconformists had charged that the congregations were not interested in the church services. The poor who found it necessary to attend in order to secure the poor relief were the only loyal members of the fourth estate. Others, both Anglican and Nonconformist, had attended the services in order to escape being called to account as office holders. Now the new laws made this unnecessary and as a result the services often proceeded with empty seats.[20] Even the middle class were less minded to attend. This naturally strengthened the charges of immorality and wickedness. In 1702 Convocation gave an entire session to drawing up a report to the Queen upon the great evils of the time. Each house drew up its own report, but on the whole there is little difference between the two so far as they discuss the sources of evil, which were stated to be the prevalence of Socinianism, the agnosticism found especially among the Quakers, and the lessening of respect for the clergy and for religion. As to immorality, it was dismissed with a sentence deprecating its sound in the ears of the Queen.[21]

This is not to say that evils were not prevalent. Morals had been of slow growth in England and the century-long period of disorders had not helped them. The continued discussion of them just at this period, however, is not a basis for the widespread opinion of modern students of the period that conditions were growing worse.[22] No doubt all the old evils were present, but what made the church alive to them was the interest in deism and the application of reason to questions of religion, as well as the readiness of the lower class

20. Atterbury, *op. cit.*

21. Mark Pattison, "Tendencies of Religious Thought in England 1688-1750," in *Essays and Reviews*, pp. 313 ff.

22. J. H. Overton, *Life in the English Church*, pp. 213 ff.; J. Woodward, *An Account of the Rise and Progress of the Religious Societies in the City of London*, pp. 69 ff.

to take advantage of the Act of Toleration and absent themselves from services within the church. This was dishearten-
ing to the clergy and the church was unprepared to cope with
it.   As to the middle class, the Revolution had put new
emphasis upon commerce and economics. Both conformist
and Nonconformist suffered from this emphasis and neither
understood clearly how the interest in commerce and trade
and industry was going to affect religious life. Not that
men were putting religion aside; rather, they were adding
a new interest that was bound to affect the nature of their
religious life.

This feeling at least gave an impetus to church effort, for
in the main it was always the small minority who, having
lost their cause in controversy, developed the desire to purge
the church by the destruction of the enemy. The Low-
Church especially but also many of the High-Church were
busily absorbed in efforts to build up a better and stronger
church. The spirituality of the Puritan group was shared
by the Low-Churchmen and was slowly recognized and seized
upon by High-Churchmen. Under Charles II the Puritan
Sabbath had been established by law. Efforts to strengthen
and widen the influence of the church by persuasion were
continuous, and with the Puritans of the Anglican church
in charge of her organization under William and Mary, the
evils of pluralism and absenteeism were much reduced.
Bishops were obliged to reside in their dioceses and to follow
a regular routine of visitation, to give greater oversight to
the work of the parish priests and vicars, and to be responsible for all candidates ordained until they had work and pay
enough to care for themselves.[23]

Under Charles II the first lay society was formed to aid
the clergy in care of the parish. Dr. Horneck gathered together the young men of his parish in London and organized

23. J. W. Legg, *English Church Life*, p. 338; Lucy Aikin, *Life of
Joseph Addison*, I, 67. A few of the most popular pamphlets had passed
the thirtieth edition.

what was to be for a long time one of the most effective means of combating the evil tendencies present in society. Under William, the Archbishop of Canterbury gave the society his approval, and it became the Society for the Reformation of Manners.[24] From 1689 its work was varied. It published and spread abroad a synopsis of the statute laws against all the popular evils together with the legal penalties for conviction. It collected funds, founded schools for the poor, endowed lectureships to encourage moral conduct, and finally organized a group of younger men to work with the constables. These men acted as informers in a more legal sense than those whom the church had employed under Charles II. They gave their time without pay, rounded up habitual swearers and drunkards, informed upon and closed bawdy houses, rescued youths and women from the hands of the evilly disposed, and, to judge from the number of arrests and convictions, must have aided materially in creating a new respect for law and order. Their work led directly to the establishment in 1697 of the Society for the Promotion of Christian Knowledge, which included all religious groups, both clerics and laity. It published tracts, established parish libraries, and founded schools for religious teaching and catechising. It shortly spread over the kingdom and into Wales, and while its work was less spectacular than that of its earlier prototype, it was more lasting and probably more worth while. It republished some of the outstanding popular works of which the renewed editions bear witness to its great usefulness.[25]

Out of this organization grew the sister society, the Society for the Propagation of the Gospel in Foreign Parts, which betokened the spiritual life of the church in that it had become aware of the common brotherhood of man, and which was the forerunner of foreign missionary societies of future

24. See injunctions given to the archbishop and bishops for preserving the unity and purity of the Christian faith, *Calendar of State Papers, Domestic*, 1695, p. 391.   25. Overton, *op. cit.*, Ch. V.

religious bodies. Thus conformity was taking on many of the characteristics of the religious life which Puritanism had fostered. The dominance of Low-Church influence aided materially in so guiding the life of the church as to accept the Nonconformist for what he was, and did much to lessen the antagonism between the two groups. Yet it cannot be said that the Low-Churchmen ever really liked the presence of Nonconformity or accepted the Puritan groups as equal religious bodies with themselves.

With the death of Mary, hostility to William and to the Nonconformists became more pronounced. A number of irresponsible churchmen began to preach and to write and agitate against Nonconformity. The cry of "the church in danger" became the rallying point and was debated on several occasions in the House of Lords. The first matter of general interest was the question of occasional conformity. That Baxter and many of the Presbyterian group had followed and advised this practice from 1660 made no difference. That the matter in no way touched the High-Churchmen, who now refused to accept the authority of the state over the church, made no difference. The practice strengthened the dissenters since it enabled them to sit in Parliament and to guide the affairs of the municipalities, and this fact was enough for the High-Churchmen. During the last years of William's reign the controversy raged as violently as it had under Charles II. Not all the dissenters supported occasional conformity. Defoe, especially, condemned the practice on logical grounds and objected to it as weakening the spiritual nature of the dissenters' cause. The Baptists for a long time had forbidden their members to enter an Anglican church for communion, and it was clear that the question would sooner or later produce a crisis. So it was also over the question of Convocation. In 1690 Convocation was dissolved on its refusal to make any approach toward comprehension and especially because of its belligerent attitude, and had not met for a decade. Arguments and pamphlets appeared defending the rights of Convocation as against the King's authority, its right to meet even against the King's wishes.[26] In 1700 William called it on the advice of his council. The lower house at once took the bit in its teeth and proceeded to act independently of the upper house. After a period of wrangling it was prorogued and did not meet again under William.

The Jacobite leanings of the High Church, its refusal to be led by the Low-Churchmen in high office, made it very clear that the majority of the Anglican ministry had repented of their support of the Revolution and were prepared to condemn that act and along with it the Act of Toleration and all recognition of the legality of Nonconformity. The church was ready for the battle and looked to the Queen as a High-Church advocate to help it have its way.

Anne on her accession promised to maintain the Toleration Act but treated the committee of the Nonconformist clergy who presented the good wishes of the dissenters with marked disdain. The High-Churchmen saw that their program was clearly to accept the Queen's position, to continue to agitate such problems as would not create a crisis, and to await events. The master mind in this program was Atterbury, who was soon made Bishop of Rochester by Anne, and with him were associated a group of men of small minds, of whom Sacheverell was the most effective and most bold.

The first problem to present itself was that of occasional conformity. The bill was presented in 1702, again in 1703, again in 1704, and again in 1705. In each year the House passed the bill only to have it thrown out by the Lords with the help of the Low-Church bishops. The High Church was able to rally its forces in 1706 when the question of union with Scotland came up, an issue that it could confidently op-

26. Francis Atterbury had been busy for some years promoting the idea that Convocation was not dependent upon the call of the King, and in the session of 1701 the independence of the lower house was especially emphasized. The disagreement of the two houses produced their dissolution.

pose with the old cry of "the church in danger" from the
Presbyterian additions to the Lords and Commons. The
Queen, having set her heart on union, dismissed Convocation
to get rid of this agitation, and the bill for union passed.
The success of the bill made stronger the case for exclusion
of dissenters from office, and in 1711 the occasional conformity bill was passed, the Whig Lords supporting it to
secure a place in the government; but their support availed
them nothing.[27]   Fearing to attack the Toleration Act
directly, the church then conceived the idea of arriving at its
goal by enacting the Schism Act, which Bolingbroke believed would not only destroy the Nonconformist monoply
of education but would enable the Anglicans to train the dissenters' children and thus through their control of education
eventually destroy the enemies of the church.[28]   Fortunately
for the Nonconformists, Anne's life was near its end and the
law which was to become effective in 1714 found the Queen
dead.   The law, set aside until the King was installed, was
later withdrawn, and Nonconformity was established by the
long Whig control under the Georges.   Even the Occasional
Conformity Act was nullified by the passing of a yearly act
to indemnify those who came under its penalty.

The long struggle for the religious freedom of the individual was won only with the coming of the first George.
The Tory party for the time being, along with High-Church
activity, was in abeyance.   Bishop Atterbury with others
joined the political leaders abroad, and controversy over the
presence of the Nonconformist group gradually turned toward other matters of which the church, as always, found
plenty.   The sects had won their right to liberty of conscience; they had been a strong factor in securing the liberties
of Englishmen against an arbitrary and irresponsible execu-
tive, and they would still continue to carry on the evolution
of that democratic spirit which the "Glorious Revolution"
had seemed to foreshadow.

27. Pickering, *Statutes*, XII, 279.   28. *Ibid.*, XIII, 70.

VII

CONCLUSIONS

THE PERIOD of the Restoration in one respect was similar
to the early Stuart period in that the monarch made full
use of the established church to support and further the theory
of the absolute form of government. Charles II, more
astute than his father, was certainly no less inclined to establish so far as possible the powers of the King over the Parliament, the church and the courts. Had his brother been as
able, the efforts to withstand the king's desire must have been
far more difficult and prolonged. The struggle that lasted
from 1660 to 1685 makes it clear that a despot with the full
use of despotic methods and a clear sense of the desired end
can easily imperil, if he cannot destroy, the liberties of a
person and a people.

The splendid intellectual defense of liberty set forth by
Milton and accepted by many of the intellectual leaders,
lay and clerical, as well as the practical effort to apply it by
Cromwell, was largely nullified by the desires of both the
Low-Churchmen and the Presbyterians who rejected the
theory and practice of toleration for a modification of the
Anglican ritual that would meet the wishes of the great
majority and establish a state church outside of whose pale
a limited group would stand, with the chance that in the
end all would have been included or eliminated.

It was most unfortunate for religious toleration that throughout the reign of Charles II the leadership in the Anglican church was held by the conservative, high Anglican group, which set the policy and shaped all church legislation. During the early years of this reign the Low-Churchmen aided or acquiesced in persecution since political intrigues at this time were so generally associated with radical Nonconformity. Moreover, the Low-Churchmen in practical church administration had little sympathy with Nonconformity, especially with the Presbyterian type, because they thought that Presbyterian objection to forms and ceremonies was directed toward unessentials, and was therefore due largely to stubbornness. It should be noticed, too, that as the Restoration proceeded the Anglican leadership tended toward the Laudian philosophy and the Low-Churchmen found it necessary to compromise their intellectual liberalism in order to keep their relations with church policy intact. Just so they had fallen into line with Laud's program earlier, although entirely opposed to it in their thinking. Laud had found not the clergy but the laity recalcitrant. The later Stuart period proves how effective such control may be when led by a determined group. There was a steady progress toward the program first enunciated by Laud and a continued acquiescence if not support by the liberal Anglican group, who, when challenged, as were Stillingfleet and Tenison, made haste to reaffirm their allegiance to the church authority. Even had the King succeeded in his efforts to secure such economic support as would have made unnecessary the calling of a parliament and could he have extended his efforts for the advancement of the interests of the trading classes, it is not clear that the course of English liberty would have been maintained. It was fortunate that the strong and intelligent leadership of the Presbyterian group tended under persecution to put emphasis upon toleration and so to aid and strengthen the Nonconformist groups as the reign of James brought to their support the constitutionalists, and finally, at the important moment, the Anglican organization which saw itself about to be sacrificed to the King's intention to establish Roman Catholicism. The reign of Anne emphasized the precarious position of toleration in the face of an intelligent, determined effort of the High Church to destroy it.

With the coming of George I, the Puritan in a substantial sense had made clear his contributions to the course of English historical development. While his Nonconformity was still, before the law, a mark of inferiority in civil and political affairs and would remain so for a century more, he had won his main contention, had kept faithfully the aims and spirit with which he began the struggle, and had been chastened and spiritualized by suffering.

In describing the course of Puritanism under the later Stuarts, there has been too little opportunity to give emphasis to its unity with the earlier period of the movement. Yet this is very necessary if one wishes to evaluate the movement as a whole. The English Reformation, unlike the general movement of the Reformation on the Continent, harked back to the historical development of English liberty through the long course of the nation's history. From the time of King John and the Charter of Liberties, or, to follow Bishop Stubbs, since the Anglo-Saxon period, the idea of the defense of the people's liberty by law to which king, noble, and church, as well as the common man must bow, was ever profoundly present. The whole course of the Reformation was in close accord with and followed the pattern of this historical development.

Thus in the effort to maintain the historical continuity of individual right against the state and the dynasty, and to secure the religious liberties of the individual, the Puritan began his peculiar struggle against the first Stuart king. It is unnecessary to contend that this larger issue was always clear even to the leaders or that it was ever clearly recognized in its larger aspect by the followers of the movement. Yet there is from the beginning of the century a very general stirring of opposition to Stuart claims that spreads far beyond and far deeper than those elements which James I drove into Separatism. As has been contended, the greater body of this opposition remained within the Anglican organization. Such laymen as John Selden, Sir Thomas Browne, Lucius Carey, Lord Herbert of Cherbury, with many others, clearly recognized not only the broader aspect of the problem but as well the false position in which the church under Laud's direction was placing itself, and did not hesitate to speak out for the principle of freedom of conscience. So also, the larger part of the 20,000 Englishmen who left England under Charles I were Puritans who had no mind to accept the tyranny of Laud and the prospect of absolutism which the eleven years of Charles's council government foreshadowed. Even on the clerical side, the writings of Hales, Chillingworth, Usher and others were to establish within the Anglican organization this idea of religious liberty which was to be a steadily growing influence through the period of Nonconformist persecution under the later Stuarts and without which Nonconformity must have found it well-nigh impossible to sustain its position.

There was another fundamental concept in this struggle that links it to the past in England's religious life as well as to all the future of English history. Mr. J. W. Bready, in his *England Before and After Wesley*, wrote: "I am forced by pressure of evidence to the conclusion that the democratic and cultural heritage of the modern English-speaking world is much more a spiritual than a political or an economic achievement. . . . and that the Evangelical Revival, which was the heir of Puritanism was the true nursing mother of the spirit and character values that have created and sustained free institutions throughout the English-speaking world." The period of persecution greatly emphasized and chastened the spiritual character of Puritanism. Religion became less a matter of theology and more completely a part of life, of thinking and living. Under persecution there was developed a readiness to succor distress—the Nonconformist poor were not fed by the tithe. Nonconformists' generosity and fair dealing won the respect even of their opponents. Their interest in education, first for their own needs and later for the poor, was a distinct national contribution, while a common suffering helped to eliminate from their minds the strong class distinctions of the time. Only those who were ready to suffer for their convictions would be likely to forego safety and convenience of membership in the established church.

No one can review the lives of the great Puritan leaders—Goudge, the apostle to the Welsh, Bunyan, writing his great religious allegory in prison where he spent twelve years of his life, Baxter, with his clear mind and great controversial ability, and Calamy, refusing high office in the Anglican church, or Howe, clear-sighted and kindly, a man who would have gone far in the state church—such lives no one can review without acknowledging the spiritual character and the love of truth which upheld and strengthened these men and thousands of others, their companions in a great adventure. Nor can one fail to see how their influence spread among all classes. For forty years England had witnessed their work and suffering while the organized state and church were using every legal means to destroy them. Men had lost their property and had been banished or had fled from the kingdom, had gone to prison, and in many cases had died there; yet they had kept the faith and the purity of their lives. Charged with treason, rebellion, lawlessness, crime, and immorality, they had become respected for their integrity which gave such charges the lie. From and with the Puritan, the evangelical group of the next century took the torch of liberty and of spirituality to bear it onward until its great value to the individual and to society was comprehended by the England that was later to become Victorian England.

If Puritanism put emphasis upon the spiritual and moral foundations of the individual life, it also led the way toward a grasp of the social possibilities in a religion which put little emphasis upon organization and much upon character. It is remarked of the reign of Anne that the most notable feature in religion was the development and rapid growth of guilds and societies organized among the laity to aid the church to combat evil and to train the young men by giving them responsibility and by this means to widen and to strengthen the influence of the clergy.

It was from the Nonconformist that England received her first lessons in the value of education. So widespread was this recognition that the nobility and even the clergy of the established church were led to choose Nonconformist schools for their sons, and later to vie with the Nonconformists in the organization of schools for the poor. The most telling point of attack upon Nonconformity during Anne's reign was the academies, seminaries and private schools that were organized by the Puritans first under Charles II to supply an educated clergy when Nonconformists were shut out from Oxford and Cambridge, and later to provide a means toward the support of the laity and finally to train their own poor in order to prepare them to make their way in a generally hostile world. How much of the intellectual activity of the eighteenth century was due to the impetus given to education by these Puritan schools it would be worth while to know. The Anglican clergy certainly gave them great recognition when they laid the evils of the use of reason in matters of religion to the Puritan schools, even though both conformist and Nonconformist were guilty.

In the matter of charity, too, the Nonconformists led the way. Their leadership was partly due to the need resulting from the rule that only those who attended the parish church could receive aid from the tithe, and partly due to the nature of their religious teaching as well as the need to sustain their members. Those who were imprisoned needed succor as well as those whose profession or business was made impossible by persecution, and ere long the habit spread to the needy wherever found. After 1689 the numbers of the needy grew apace, since the legal urge to attend the parish church was withdrawn. Their plight was greatly emphasized by the slowness with which the state met the problem of poor relief during a period when great changes were taking place in the economic world. It should not be overlooked that the High-Church Nonconformists very soon saw the same necessity of meeting the social problems of those who followed them from the church. Wesley testified to the influence which William Law's *Serious Call to a Holy Life* had made upon him, while his whole life and work were a testimony to the great value of religion as applied to the social need. The evangelical spirit was abroad in the eighteenth century. To be sure it developed slowly, but it had first to make over men's ideas before it could find out proper methods of procedure. It should be remembered, however, that the impetus which was to revolutionize and modernize religion had come from Puritanism, the application of faith in God to man's relation to his fellows. The social application had to wait a century's development, but the Puritan had made it clear that there could be no turning back from the course. One is inclined to believe that the failure to recognize the social need in religion had much to do with the emphasis upon the evils of the time in the early part of the century. In reading the complaints of Convocation as well as of individuals, one finds always a great emphasis upon the evil effects of the Puritan influence in drawing adherents from church attendance. In this the charge is specific. It is a testimony to the habit of non-attendance at church which drew men to the tavern, to low sports and to all the resultant laxness.

There is no mistaking the prevalence of swearing and drunkenness and the existence of bawdy houses, mention of

which appeared constantly in the charges made by the Society
for the Reformation of Manners after 1688. The charges
were made from time to time under Charles and James,
but the character of the court made a jest of laws passed
by Parliament. No reasonable proof was ever produced
that these evils existed among the Puritan group and the
falsity of such accusations made by churchmen became
clearer and more definite after the Revolution of 1688.
Under Charles and James there was a definite lack of preaching against social ills, though it occasionally was heard in
the court sermons. With the coming of the Restoration
there was certainly a definite slackening in the effort to control crime, and immorality grew in court and out of it.

The fact remains, however, that the recognition of these
evils and the pronounced effort to overcome them awaited
the period when the Low-Churchmen were given greater
prominence in leadership and the evangelical influence began
to be felt in national life. Pattison in discussing this problem,
after quoting Hallam at length on the evils of irreligion,
asserts that outside of "Ministers and Privy Council religion
had a firm hold upon the people."[1] So also Legg in his
English Church Life[2] testifies to the popularity of the *Spec-
tator* which made no mention of infidelity and in its irony
and satire spared popular evils. Samuel Johnson later called
attention to the library of the English country house as con-
sisting of the Bible, religious tracts, and devotional books.[3]
Certainly it may be said that Puritanism by 1715 had distinctly marked the pathway to the Victorian morality which
put its stress upon the application of religion to the every-
day life of the people. How strongly this was felt even
up to the French Revolution is seen in Burke's declaration
that religion was the moral foundation of the state and that
the attempt to weaken religion was aimed at the state's
destruction.

1. Pattison, "Tendencies of Religious Thought in England," *Essays and
Reviews*, p. 313.   2. Pp. 44 ff.
   3. John C. Bailey, *Dr. Johnson and his Circle*, p. 27.

SELECTED BIBLIOGRAPHY

A. CONTEMPORARY MATERIALS

I. OFFICIAL PUBLICATIONS, PUBLIC DOCUMENTS, ETC.

Calendar of State Papers, Domestic. Volumes for the reigns of Charles II, James II, and William III.

Calendar of State Papers, Venetian. Volumes for the reign of Charles II.

Cardwell, Edward. *Documentary Annals of the Reformed Church of England from the Year 1546 to the Year 1716.* 2 vols., Oxford, 1839.

[Charles II]. *His Majesty's Declaration to his Loving Subjects, December 26, 1662.* Published by advice of his Privy Council. London, 1662.

———. *His Majesty's Gracious Speech together with the Lord Keeper's to both Houses of Parliament, April 13, 1675.* Published by His Majesty's special command. London, 1675.

Debates of the House of Commons from the Year 1667 to the Year 1694. Collected by the Hon. Anchitel Grey. 10 vols., London, 1769.

Hall, Peter. *Reliquiae Liturgicae: Documents connected with the Liturgy of the Church of England.* . . . 5 vols., Bath, 1847.

Harleian Society. *Registers.* London, 1877.

Historical Manuscripts Commission. *Fourteenth Report,* App. II: *Manuscripts of the Duke of Portland,* Vol. III (Harley Papers).

———. *Report on the Manuscripts of the Earl of Egmont.* 2 vols.

Journals of the House of Commons. Volumes for the reigns of Charles II and James II.

Journals of the House of Lords. Volumes for the reigns of
Charles II and James II.

The Parliamentary History of England. Ed. by William Cobbett.
36 vols., London, 1806-1820.

Revised Statutes [1235-1878]. 18 vols., 1870-1885.

*Statutes at Large from Magna Charta to the Seventh Year of
King George the Second.* Ed. by William Hawkins. 6 vols.,
London, 1735.

Statutes at Large from Magna Charta to . . . 1761. Ed. by
Danby Pickering. 24 vols., Cambridge, 1762.

*To the Right Reverend and Reverend the Bishops and Clergy
of the Province of Canterbury to be assembled in Convocation
at Westminster A. D. 1690: The humble Petition of many
Divines and others of the Classical, Congregational, and other
Persuasions in the Name of themselves and Brethren both of
Old England and New, who have born Witness to the
Truth in the Day of Trial.* London, 1689.

Turner, G. Lyon, ed. *Original Records of early Nonconformity under Persecution and Indulgence.* 3 vols., London, 1911-
1914.

*The Visitation of the County Palatine of Lancaster, made in the
Year 1664-1665.* Ed. by F. R. Raines. 3 parts, Chetham
Society, Vols. LXXXIV, LXXXV, and LXXXVIII, 1872-
1873.

[William III]. *Directions to our Archbishop and Bishops for the
Preserving of Unity in the Church and Purity of the Christian
Faith concerning the Holy Trinity.* By His Majesty's special
Command. London, 1695.

Woodhouse, A. S. P., ed. *Puritanism and Liberty: Being the
Army Debates (1647-1649) from the Clarke Manuscript
with supplementary Documents.* Selected and edited with an
Introduction. London, 1938.

II. BIOGRAPHIES, DIARIES, HISTORIES, MEMOIRS

Baxter, Richard. *Reliquiae Baxterianae: Or Mr. Richard Baxter's Narrative of the most memorable Passages of his Life
and Times.* Faithfully published from his own original Manuscript by Matthew Sylvester. London, 1696.

Birch, Thomas. *The Life of the Most Reverend Dr. John Tillotson.* . . . London, 1752.

Brockbank, The Reverend Thomas. *Diary and Letter Book, 1671-1709.* Ed. by Richard Trappes-Lomax. Chetham Society, Vol. LXXXIX, New Series, 1930.

Burnet, Gilbert. *History of his own Time.* 6 vols., London, 1833.

Calamy, Edmund. *An Abridgement of Mr. Baxter's History of his Life and Times, with an Account of many others of those worthy Ministers who were ejected after the Restoration.* . . . London, 1702.

———. *An Account of the Ministers, Lecturers, Masters, and Fellows of Colleges, and Schoolmasters who were ejected and silenced after the Restoration in 1660 by or before the Act for Uniformity.* Second edition, London, 1710.

———. *An Historical Account of my own Life, with some Reflections on the Times I have lived in.* Ed. by J. T. Rutt, 2 vols., 1829.

———. *The Nonconformist's Memorial, being an Account of the Ministers who were ejected or silenced after the Restoration.* . . . Originally written by . . . Edmund Calamy, now abridged and corrected . . . by Samuel Palmer. 2 vols., London, 1775.

Evelyn, John. *Diary.* Ed. by William Bray. 4 vols., London, 1879.

Luttrell, Narcissus. *A Brief Historical Relation of State Affairs from September, 1678 to April, 1714.* 6 vols., Oxford, 1857.

Neal, Daniel. *The History of the Puritans.* 2 vols., New York, 1858.

Newcome, Henry. *The Diary of the Rev. Henry Newcome from September 30, 1661 to September 29, 1663.* Ed. by Thomas Heywood. Chetham Society, 1849.

Parr, Richard. *The Life of the Most Reverend Father in God, James Usher . . . with a Collection of Three Hundred Letters.* . . . London, 1686.

Pepys, Samuel. *Diary.* Ed. by Henry B. Wheatley. 9 vols., New York, 1893-1899.

Thoresby, Ralph. *Diary and Correspondence, 1677-1724.* Ed. by Joseph Hunter. 4 vols., London, 1830-1831.

III. SERMONS, TRACTS, TREATISES, ETC.

A., F. *A Letter from a Gentleman of Gray's Inn to a Justice of the Peace in the Country explaining the Act of Uniformity in that Part which doth concern unlicensed Preachers.* London, 1662.

Addison, Lancelot. *A Modest Plea for the Clergy, wherein is briefly considered the Original, Antiquity, Necessity. Together with the spurious and genuine Occasion of their present Contempt.* . . . London, 1677.

Allen, William. *A Persuasive to Peace and Unity among Christians.* . . . London, 1672.

Allestree, Richard. *The Causes of the Decay of Christian Piety: Or an impartial Survey of the Ruins of Christian Religion undermined by Unchristian Practice.* . . . London, 1668.

Atterbury, Francis. *A Representation of the Present State of Religion.* London, 1711.

B., J. *Certain Proposals humbly offered for the Preservation and Continuance of the truly reformed Protestant Religion.* . . . London, 1674.

B., W. D. *A Letter to the Right Worshipful T. S., a Member of the Honorable House of Commons, with some Remarks upon the intended Act against Nonconformists, in order to Moderation.* London, 1675.

Barret, William. *Nonconformists vindicated from Abuses put upon them by Mr. Durel and Scrivener.* . . . London, 1679.

Barrington, John Shute, Viscount. *An Essay upon the Interest of England in respect to Protestants dissenting from the Church of England.* London, 1701.

Baxter, Richard. *An Apology for the Nonconformist Ministry.* . . . London, 1681.

———. *English Nonconformity as under Charles II and James II truly stated and argued.* London, 1689.

———. *The Nonconformists' Plea for Peace: Or an Account of their Judgment in certain Things in which they are Misunderstood.* London, 1679.

————. *A Petition for Peace, with the Reformation of the Liturgy as it was presented to the Right Reverend Bishops by the Divines appointed by His Majesty's Commission.* . . . London, 1661.

————. *The Poor Husbandman's Advocate to Rich Racking Landlords, written in Compassion especially of their Souls and of the Land.* . . . The Reverend Richard Baxter's last treatise copied from the manuscript . . . and edited by Frederick J. Powicke . . . with an Introduction by the late George Unwin. Reprint from the *John Rylands Library Bulletin*, X (1926), 163-218.

————. *The Right Method for a settled Peace of Conscience and spiritual Comfort. In thirty-two Directions written for the use of a Troubled Friend.* Fourth edition, London, 1699.

————. *A Sermon of Repentance preached before the Honorable House of Commons assembled in Parliament at Westminster at their late solemn Fast for the Settlement of these Nations, April 30, 1660.* London, 1660.

Bennet, Thomas. *An Answer to the Dissenters' Pleas for Separation.* Third edition, Cambridge, 1701.

Blake, Martin. *An Earnest Plea for Peace and Moderation, in a Sermon.* . . . London, 1661.

Bolde, Samuel. *A Plea for Moderation toward Dissenters.* . . . London, 1682.

Bradshaw, William. *English Puritanism: The main Opinions of the rigidest Sort of those that are called Puritans in the Realm of England.* Third edition, London, 1660.

Bramhall, John. *Vindication of Himself and the Episcopal Clergy from the Presbyterian Charge of Popery.* . . . London, 1672.

Buckingham, George Villiers, Duke of. *Letter to Sir Thomas Osborn, one of his Majesty's Privy Council, upon the Reading of a Book called The Present Interest of England Stated.* London, 1672.

————. *Letter to the Unknown Author of a Paper entitled, A short Answer to . . . the Duke of Buckingham's Paper concerning Religion, Toleration, and Liberty of Conscience.* London, 1685.

Burnet, Gilbert. *The Case of Compulsion in Matters of Religion stated.* . . . London, 1688.

————. *A Sermon preached . . . to the Societies for Reformation of Manners, the twenty-fifth of March, 1700.* London, 1700.

Burroughs, Edward. *The Case of Free Liberty of Conscience in the Exercise of Faith and Religion.* . . . London, 1661.

Calamy, Edmund. *Eli trembling for the Fear of the Ark: A Sermon preached at St. Mary Aldermanbury December 28, 1662 . . . upon the preaching of which he was committed Prisoner to the Gaol of Newgate.* Oxford, 1662/3.

Calamy, Edmund, and others. *An Exact Collection of Farewell Sermons preached by the late London Ministers: viz., Mr. Calamy, Mr. Watson, Mr. Jacomb, Mr. Case, Mr. Sclater, Mr. Baxter, Mr. Jenkin, Mr. Manton, Mr. Lye, and Mr. Collins.* . . . London, 1662.

C[are], G[eorge]. *Liberty of Conscience Asserted and Vindicated.* . . . London, 1689.

Carr, Alan. *A Peaceable Moderator: Or some plain Considerations to give Satisfaction to such as stand disaffected to our Book of Common Prayer established by Authority, clearing it from the Aspersions of Popery.* London, 1665.

Clarke, Samuel. Dr. Clarke's Book of Common Prayer with Manuscript Alterations in his own Hand. In the British Museum MS Collections.

Clarendon, Edward Hyde, Earl of. *Two Letters written by Edward Earl of Clarendon late Lord High Chancellor of England: One to his Royal Highness the Duke of York, the other to the Duchess, occasioned by her embracing the Roman Catholic Religion.* Harleian Miscellany, VII, 430-35, London, 1810.

Coke, Roger. *A Treatise wherein is demonstrated that the Church and State of England are in equal Danger with the Trade of it.* London, 1671.

Compton, Henry. *Bishop Compton's Charge to the Clergy of the London Diocese at his Visitation.* London, 1696.

Cooper, Anthony Ashley. *A Letter from a Parliament Man to his Friend concerning the Proceedings of the House of Commons this last Session.* . . . London, 1675.

Corbet, John. *An Account of the Principles and Practice of several Nonconformists. . . .* London, 1682.

―――. *The Interest of England in Matters of Religion unfolded in the Solution of these three Questions: I.Q. Whether the Presbyterian Party should in Justice or Reason of State be Rejected and Depressed or Protected and Encouraged. II.Q. Whether the Presbyterian Party may be Protected and encouraged and the Episcopal not deserted nor disobliged. III.Q. Whether the Upholding of both Parties by a just and equal Accommodation be not in itself more desirable and more agreeable to the State of England than the absolute Exalting of one Party and the total Subversion of the other.* London, 1660.

―――. *The Nonconformists' Plea for Lay Communion with the Church of England. . . .* London, 1683.

Croft, Herbert. *The Naked Truth: Or, the True State of the Primitive Church. . . .* London, 1675.

―――. *A Short Discourse concerning the Reading His Majesty's late Declaration in the Churches. . . .* London, 1688.

Crook, John, and others. *Liberty of Conscience asserted and several Reasons rendered why no outward Force nor Imposition ought to be used in Matters of Faith and Religion. . . .* London, 1661.

D., W. *The Present Interest of England in Matters of Religion stated. . . .* London, 1688.

Darrell, William. *The Layman's Opinion sent in a private Letter to a Considerable Divine of the Church of England.* London, 1687.

Defoe, Daniel. *An Enquiry into the Occasional Conformity of Dissenters in Cases of Preferment. . . .* London, 1697.

―――. *A New Discovery of an old Intrigue: A Satire leveled at Treachery and Ambition calculated to the Nativity of the Rapparee Plot and the Modesty of the Jacobite Clergy.* London, 1691.

―――. *The Poor Man's Plea to all the Proclamations, Declarations, Acts of Parliament, &c. which have been, or shall be made, or published, for a Reformation of Manners and Suppressing Immorality in the Nation.* London, 1698.

————. *The Shortest Way with the Dissenters: Or Proposals for the Establishment of the Church.* London, 1702.

DeLaume, Thomas. *A Plea for the Nonconformists, giving the true State of the Dissenters' Case; and how far the Conformists' Separation from the Church of Rome for their Popish Superstitions and Traditions introduced into the Service of God justifies the Nonconformists' Separation from them for the Same. . . .* London, 1684.

Dell, William. *The Increase of Popery in England since the Reformation made by King Henry VIII.* London, 1681.

Dodwell, Henry. *The Doctrine of the Church of England concerning the Independency of the Clergy on Lay Power as to those Rights of theirs which are purely spiritual, reconciled with our Oath of Supremacy. . . .* London, 1697.

E., H. *The Juryman Charged: Or a Letter to a Citizen of London, wherein is shown the true Meaning of the Statute entitled An Act to Prevent and Suppress Seditious Conventicles. . . .* London, 1664.

Eachard, John. *A Free and impartial Inquiry into the Causes of that very great Esteem and Honor that the Nonconforming Preachers are generally in with their Followers. . . .* London, 1673.

————. *Grounds and Occasions for the Contempt of the Clergy and Religion Enquired into.* London, 1670.

Farnworth, Richard. *Christian religious Meetings allowed by the Liturgy are no Seditious Conventicles.* London, 1664.

Fullwood, Francis. *Obedience due to the Present King, notwithstanding our Oaths to the Former. . . .* London, 1689.

Gauden, John. *Considerations touching the Liturgy of the Church of England in Reference to His Majesty's late Declaration and in order to a happy Union in Church and State.* London, 1661.

Glanvill, Joseph. *The Zealous and Impartial Protestant, showing some great but less heeded Dangers of Popery. . . .* In a Letter to a Member of Parliament. London, 1681.

Goodman, John. *A Serious and Compassionate Inquiry into Causes of the present Neglect and Contempt of the Protestant Religion and the Church of England, with several seasonable*

Considerations offered to all English Protestants, tending to persuade them to a Compliance with and Conformity to the Religion and Government of this Church as it is established by the Laws of the Kingdom. . . . London, 1674.

Gother, John. *An Agreement between the Church of England and Church of Rome, evinced from the Concentration of some of her Sons with their Brethren the Dissenters.* London, 1687.

Grove, Robert. *A Persuasive to Communion with the Church of England.* London, 1683.

Halifax, George Savile, Marquis of. *Miscellanies by the most noble George Lord Savile, late Marquis and Earl of Halifax.* . . . Third edition, London, 1717.

Harrington, James. *Some Reflections upon a Treatise called Pietas Romana & Parisiensis.* . . . *To which are added a Vindication of Protestant Charity . . . and a Defence.* . . . Oxford, 1688.

Hart, Richard (pseud.). *Parish Churches turned into Conventicles by serving God therein and worshiping him otherwise than according to the established Liturgy and Practice of the Church of England.* . . . London, 1683.

Henchman, Richard. *A Peace Offering in the Temple: Or a seasonable Plea for Unity among dissenting Brethren.* . . . London, 1661.

Herbert, George. *A Priest to the Temple: Or the Country Parson, his Character and Rule of Holy Life.* Second edition. London, 1671.

Humphrey, John. *A Defence of the Proposition, or some Reasons rendered why the Nonconformist Minister who comes to his Parish Church and Common Prayer cannot yet yield to other Things that are enjoined without some Moderation.* . . . London, 1668.

———. *The Two Steps of a Nonconformist Minister made by him in order to the Obtaining his Liberty of Preaching in Public; with an Appendix about coming to Church in Respect of the People.* London, 1684.

Jane, William. *A Letter to a Friend containing some Queries about the New Commission for making Alterations in the*

Liturgy, Canons, &c., of the Church of England. London, 1689.

Jones, James. *Nonconformity not inconsistent with Loyalty: Or Protestant Dissenters no seditious or disloyal Sectaries. . . .* London, 1684.

[Juxon, William]. Χαρις καί Ειρήνη: *Or some Considerations upon the Act of Uniformity, with an Expedient for the Satisfaction of the Clergy within the Province of Canterbury. . . .* London, 1662.

Kidder, Richard. *Charity Directed: Or the Way to give Alms to the greater Advantage.* London, 1677.

———. *The Judgment of private Discretion in Matters of Religion defended. . . .* London, 1687.

Law, William. *William Law's Defence of Church Principles: Three Letters to the Bishop of Bangor.* Edited by J. O. Nash and Charles Gore. London, 1893.

Leslie, Charles. *Querela Temporum: Or the Danger of the Church of England. . . .* London, 1695.

L'Estrange, Roger. *Considerations and Proposals in order to the Regulation of the Press: Together with diverse Instances of treasonous and seditious Pamphlets proving the Necessity thereof.* London, 1663.

———. *The Observator Defended. . . .* London, 1685.

Littleton, Adam. *The Church's Peace asserted upon a civil Account. . . .* London, 1669.

Locke, John. *A Letter concerning Toleration.* London, 1689.

———. *Two Treatises of Government: In the former, the false Principles and Foundation of Sir Robert Filmer and his Followers are detected and overthrown. The Latter is an Essay concerning the true Original, Extent, and End of Civil Government.* London, 1689.

———. *A Vindication of the Reasonableness of Christianity as delivered in the Scriptures. . . .* London, 1695.

Long, Thomas. *Mr. Hale's Treatise of Schism examined and censured. . . . To which are added Mr. Baxter's Arguments for Conformity, wherein the most material Passages of the Treatise of Schism are answered.* London, 1678.

————. *Vox Cleri: Or the Sense of the Clergy concerning the making of Alterations in the established Liturgy.* London, 1690.

Lucas, Richard. *Practical Christianity: Or an Account of the Holiness which the Gospel enjoins, with the Motives to it and the Remedies it proposes against Temptations. . . .* London, 1678.

Manby, William. *Some Considerations toward Peace and Quietness in Religion, in Answer to the Question whether the Multitude are fit Readers of the Scripture.* London, 1680.

[Mather, Increase]. *A Letter of Advice to the Churches of the Nonconformists in the English Nation.* London, 1700.

Maurice, Henry. *The Lawfulness of taking the new Oaths asserted.* London, 1689.

————. *A Letter out of the Country to a Member of this present Parliament occasioned by a late Letter to a Member of the House of Commons concerning the Bishops lately in the Tower. . . .* London, 1689.

Monck, George. *A Collection of several Letters and Declarations sent . . . unto King Charles II, the Lord Lambert, the Lord Fleetwood, and the rest of the General Council of Officers of the Army; as also unto that Part of the Parliament called the Rump, the Committee of Safety, the Lord Mayor and Common Council, the Congregated Churches in and about London.* London, 1660.

Nalson, John. *A Letter from a Jesuit at Paris to his Correspondent in London, showing the most effectual Way to ruin the Government and Protestant Religion.* London, 1679.

————. *The Present Interest of England: Or a Confutation of the Whiggish Conspirators' Antinomian Principle, showing from Reason and Experience the Ways to make the Government safe, the King great, the People happy, Money plentiful, and Trade flourish.* London, 1684.

Newnam, Richard. *The Complaint of English Subjects, delivered in two Parts. . . . The Complaint of the Poor, Middle, and Meanest Sorts of Subjects, concerning their bodily Assistance. . . . The True Christian's Complaint against Vice and Wickedness, for the Good of their Souls' Health. . . .* London, 1699.

Norris, John. *Practical Discourses on several Divine Subjects: viz. Of Religious Discourses in common Conversation, Of the Fear of Death, Concerning the Extent of Christ's Satisfaction, Of Walking by Faith, Concerning Charity to the Poor, Concerning the right Use of the World, Concerning the successive Vanity of Human Life.* . . . London, 1697.

Nourse, Peter. *Practical Discourses on several Subjects, being some select Homilies of the Church of England put into a new Method and modern Style and fitted to common Use.* London, 1705.

P., B. *A Modest and Peaceable Letter concerning Comprehension.* . . . London, 1668.

Patrick, Simon. *A Friendly Debate betwixt two Neighbors, the one a Conformist, the other a Nonconformist.* London, 1668.
————. *The Parable of the Pilgrim.* . . . London, 1668.

Pearse, Edward. *The Conformist's Plea for the Nonconformists: Or a just and compassionate Representation of the present State and Condition of the Nonconformists as to I. The Greatness of their Sufferings. II. The Hardness of their Case. III. Reasonableness and Equity of their Desires and Proposals. IV. Qualifications and Worth of their Persons. V. Peaceableness of their Behavior. VI. The Church's Prejudice by their Exclusion, &c.* Humbly submitted to Authority by a beneficed Minister, and a regular Son of the Church of England. London, 1681.

Penington, Isaac. *Concerning Persecution: Which is the Afflicting or Punishing that which is Good under the Pretense of its being Evil.* London, 1661.

Penn, William. *Good Advice to the Church of England, Roman Catholic, and Protestant Dissenter.* . . . London, 1687.

[Penn, William]. *A Letter from a Gentleman in the Country to his Friends in London upon the Subject of the Penal Laws and Tests.* London, 1687.

Penn, William. *The Present Interest of England discovered, with Honor to the Prince and Safety to the People.* London, 1675.
————. *Some sober and weighty Reason against persecuting Protestant Dissenters for Difference of Opinions in Matters of Religion.* . . . London, 1682.

Perrinchief, Richard. *Samaritanism Revised and Enlarged: Or a Treatise against Comprehending, Compounding, or Tolerating several Religions and Modes of Worship in the same Church.* . . . London, 1669.

Reynall, Carew. *The true English Interest, or an Account of the chief national Improvements: In political Observations demonstrating an infallible Advance of this Nation to infinite Wealth and Greatness, Trade, and Populacy with Employment and Preferment for all Persons.* London, 1674.

Reynolds, Edward. *The Means and Method of Healing in the Church.* . . . London, 1660.

S., J. *Doctrine of the Church of England concerning the Lord's Day, or Sunday Sabbath, as it is laid down in the Liturgy, Catechism, and Book of Homilies, vindicated from the vulgar Errors of modern Writers and settled upon the only proper and sure Basis of God's Precept to Adam and patriarchal Practice.* . . . London, 1683.

Sharp, John. *Fifteen Sermons preached on several Occasions.* Second edition, London, 1701.

Stillingfleet, Edward. *Ecclesiastical Cases relating to the Duties and Rights of the parochial Clergy.* . . . London, 1698.

———. *Irenicum: A Weapon Salve for the Church's Wounds.* . . . Second edition, London, 1662.

———. *A Letter to Mr. G. giving a true Account of the late Conference at the D. of P.* London, 1687.

———. *The Mischief of Separation: A Sermon preached at Guild Hall, May 2, 1680.* Fourth edition, London, 1687.

———. *A Rational Account of the Grounds of the Protestant Religion.* . . . London, 1665.

———. *The Unreasonableness of Separation.* . . . London, 1681.

Stockton, Owen. *A Rebuke to Informers: With a Plea for Ministers of the Gospel called Nonconformists and their Meetings.* . . . London, 1675.

Sturgeon, John. *A Plea for Toleration of Opinions and Persuasions in Matters of Religion differing from the Church of England.* . . . Humbly presented to the King's most excellent Majesty. . . . London, 1661.

Sykes, A. A. *An Answer to the Nonjurors' Charge of Schism upon the Church of England.* . . . London, 1716.

Synge, Edward. *A Gentleman's Religion with the Grounds and Reasons of it: In which the Truth of Christianity in general is vindicated, its Simplicity asserted, and some introductory Rules for the Discovering of its particular Doctrines and Precepts are proposed.* By a Private Gentleman. London, Part I, 1693. Parts II & III, 1697.

Taylor, Jeremy. *Ductor Dubitantium, or the Rule of Conscience.* . . . London, 1660.

———. *Holy Living and Holy Dying.* New edition, London, 1850.

———. *Rules and Advices to the Clergy of the Diocese of Down and Connor.* . . . London, 1663.

Temple, William. *Observations upon the United Provinces of the Netherlands, containing an account of the Rise and Progress of their State, of their Government, of their Situation, of their People and Dispositions, of their Religion, of their Trade, of their Forces and Revenues, of the Causes of their Fall in 1671.* London, 1673.

Tenison, Thomas. *An Argument for Union taken from the true Interests of those Dissenters in England who profess and call themselves Protestants.* London, 1683.

Tomkins, Thomas. *The modern Pleas for Comprehension, Toleration, and the taking away the Obligation to the Renouncing of the Covenant considered and discussed.* London, 1675.

[Usher, James]. *The Bishop of Armagh's Direction concerning the Liturgy and Episcopal Government.* London, 1642.

———. *Episcopal and Presbyterial Government conjoined. Proposed as an Expedient for the Compromising of the Differences.* . . . London, 1679.

Wake, William. *The State of the Church and Clergy of England in their Councils, Synods, Convocations, Conventions, and other public Assemblies.* . . . London, 1703.

Walwyn, William. *A Prediction of Mr. Edwards his Conversion and Recantation.* London, 1646.

Warmstry, Thomas. *A Countermine of Union to the Jesuits' Mine of Division.* . . . London, 1660.

Welwood, James. *Vindication of the present great Revolution in England: In five Letters.* . . . London, 1689.

Whitaker, Edward. *An Answer to the Order of the Middlesex Justices dated the twentieth of December last touching the Suppressing of Conventicles.* . . . London, 1682.

―――. *An Argument for Toleration and Indulgence in Relation to Differences in Opinion, both as it is the Interest of States and as a common Duty of all Christians one to another.* . . . London, 1681.

Whitby, Daniel. *A Letter from a City Minister to a Member of the high and honorable Court of Parliament concerning present Affairs: Being a Vindication of the Church of England Clergy for their Owning and Praying for King William and Queen Mary.* London, 1689.

Woodward, J. *An Account of the Rise and Progress of the Religious Societies in the City of London.* . . . Second edition, London, 1698.

―――. *The Judgment of . . . Dr. Henry Sacheverell concerning the Societies for the Reformation of Manners . . . with some Reflections thereon.* London, 1711.

IV. ANONYMOUS PAMPHLETS

The Case of Protestants in England under a Popish Prince, if any shall happen to wear the Imperial Crown. London, 1681.

The Case stated touching the Sovereign's Prerogative and the People's Liberty according to Scripture, Reason, and the Consent of our Ancestors, humbly offered to the Right Honorable General Monck and the Officers in the Army. London, 1660.

Certain Considerations tending to promote Peace and good Will among Protestants. . . . London, 1674.

Christian Unity exhorted to: Being a few Words in tender Love to all professing Christians in Old England the Land of my Nativity. . . . London, 1678.

A Collection of Papers relating to the present Juncture of Affairs in England. London, 1688. (The first of a series, twelve in all, published during 1688-1689.)

A Confession of Faith put forth by the Elders and Brethren of many Congregations. . . . London, 1677.

A Discourse between George, a true-hearted English Gentleman, and Hans, a Dutch Merchant. London, 1672.

The Dissenter's Guide, resolving Doubts and Scruples about kneeling for the Sacrament. London, 1683.

An Earnest and Compassionate Suit for Forbearance to the learned Writers of some Controversies at Present. London, 1691.

English Liberties: Or the freeborn Subject's Inheritance concerning Magna Charta, Petition of Right, Habeas Corpus Act, and other useful Statutes, with large Comments. . . . London, 1692.

English Presbytery: An Account of the main Opinions of those Ministers and People in England who go under the Name of Presbyterians. . . . London, 1680.

The Englishman: Or a Letter from a universal Friend persuading all sober Protestants to hearty and sincere Love of one another. . . . London, 1670.

Et a Dracone: Some Reflections on a Discourse Omnia a Bello Conesta, &c. London, 1672.

An Examination of the Bishops upon their Refusal of Reading His Majesty's Declaration, and the Nonconcurrence of the Church of England in Repeal of the Penal Laws and Tests, debated. London, 1688.

The Examination of the Case of the suspended Bishops in Answer to the Apology for them. London, 1690.

A Few Sober Queries upon the late Proclamation for Enforcing the Laws against Conventicles . . . and the Law renewing the Act. London, 1672.

A Friendly Conference concerning the new Oath of Allegiance to King William and Queen Mary: Wherein the Objections against taking the Oaths are impartially examined and the Reasons of Obedience confirmed, from the Writings of the profound Bishop Sanderson, and proved to agree to the Principles of the Church of England and the Laws of the Land. By a Divine of that Church. London, 1689.

A General View of our present Discontents. . . . London, 1710.

The Grand Debate between the most Reverend Bishops and the Presbyterian Divines appointed by His Sacred Majesty as Commissioners for the Review and Alteration of the Book of Common Prayer. . . . London, 1661.

The Grounds of Unity in Religion: Or an Expedient for a general Conformity and Pacification. London, 1672.

Heads of Agreement assented to by the united Ministers in and about London, formerly called Presbyterian and Congregational. . . . London, 1691.

Indulgence not to be refused, Comprehension humbly desired, the Church's Peace earnestly endeavored. . . . London, 1672.

Indulgence to tender Consciences shown to be most Reasonable and Christian. By a Minister of the Church of England. London, 1687.

A Letter from a Dissenter in the City to his Country Friend, wherein Moderation and Occasional Conformity are vindicated. London, 1705.

A Letter from a Gentleman in the City to a Friend in the Country about the Odiousness of Persecution, occasioned by the late rigorous Proceedings against sober Dissenters by certain angry Justices in the Country. London, 1677.

A Letter from a Gentleman of Gray's Inn to a Justice of the Peace in the Country explaining the Act of Uniformity. London, 1662.

A Letter from a Justice of the Peace to a Counsellor at Law concerning Conventicles. London, 1681.

A Letter to a dissenting Clergyman of the Church of England concerning the Oath of Allegiance and Obedience to the present Government. London, 1690.

A Letter to a Gentleman in Brussels containing an Account of the People's Revolt from the Crown. London, 1689.

Liberty of Conscience in its order to universal Peace impartially stated. . . . London, 1681.

The Memorial of the Church of England humbly offered to the Consideration of all true Lovers of our Church and Constitution. . . . London, 1705. (Ascribed variously to William Pittis and to J. Drake.)

The Mischief of Dissensions: Or a Persuasive to Dr. Stillingfleet . . . together with his Respondents to a seasonable Alliance from their Literal War. . . . London, 1681.

The Moderation and Loyalty of the Dissenters exemplified from the Historians and other Writers. . . . London, 1710.

A Modest Censure of an immodest Letter to a Dissenter. London, 1687.

A Modest Examination of the New Oath of Allegiance by a Divine of the Church of England. London, 1689.

The New Test of the Church of England's Loyalty examined by the Old Test of Truth and Honesty. London, 1687.

The Nonconformist's Plea for Uniformity. Being the Judgment of fourscore and four Ministers of the County Palatine of Lancaster . . . concerning Toleration and Uniformity in Matters of Religion. Together with a Resolution of this difficult Question: Whether the Penalty of the Law ought to be inflicted on those who pretend and plead Conscience in Opposition to what the Law commands. London, 1674.

A Perfect Guide for Protestant Dissenters in Case of Persecution upon any of the penal Statutes made against them. . . . London, 1682.

A Plea for Moderation: Or a Stricture on the Ecclesiastics of our Times. London, 1681.

The Reformed Papist and High Churchman. . . . London, 1681.

A Representation of the State of Christianity in England and of its Decay and Danger from Sectaries as well as Papists. London, 1674.

A Seasonable Exhortation of sundry Ministers to the People of their respective Congregations. London, 1660.

A Second Collection of Papers relating to the present Juncture of Affairs in England. London, 1688.

Several Arguments for Concessions and Alterations in the Common Prayer and in Rites and Ceremonies of the Church of England in order to a Comprehension. By a Minister of the Church of England. London, 1689.

Toleration and Liberty of Conscience considered and proved impracticable, impossible, and even in the Opinion of Dissenters Sinful and Unlawful. London, 1685.

Two Papers of Proposals concerning the Discipline and Ceremonies of the Church of England humbly presented to His Majesty by the Reverend Ministers of the Presbyterian Persuasion. London, 1661.

The Way of Peace: Or a Discourse of the dangerous Principles and Practices of some pretended Protestants. . . . London, 1680.

The Way to be Rich according to the Practice of the great Audley, who begun with two hundred Pounds in the Year 1605 and died worth four hundred thousand Pounds this instant November. London, 1662.

B. SECONDARY MATERIALS

Aiken, Lucy. *Life of Joseph Addison.* 2 vols., London, 1843.

Bailey, John C. *Dr. Johnson and his Circle.* New York, 1913.

Bebb, Evelyn D. *Nonconformity and Social and Economic Life.* London, 1935.

Bready, J. W. *England before and after Wesley: The Evangelical Revival and Social Reform.* London, 1938.

Brown, Louise. "The Religious Factors in the Convention Parliament," *English Historical Review,* XXII (1907), 51-63.

Buchan, John. *Oliver Cromwell.* London, 1934.

Clark, Henry W. *History of English Nonconformity from Wycliff to the Close of the Nineteenth Century.* 2 vols., London, 1911-1913.

Crouch, Joseph. *Puritanism and Art: An Inquiry into a Popular Fallacy.* New York, 1910.

Dobell, Percy J. *The Literature of the Restoration.* London, 1918.

Dowden, Edward. *Puritan and Anglican.* New York, 1901.

D'Oyly, George. *Life of William Sancroft.* 2 vols., London, 1821.

Fiennes, Celia. *Through England on a Side Saddle in the Time of William and Mary.* London, 1888.

Gardiner, S. R. *Cromwell's Place in History.* Third edition, London, 1897.

Gee, Henry. *The Derwentdale Plot, 1663.* Trans. Royal Hist. Soc., 3rd. ser., no. xi, 1917.

Glover, Terrot R. *Poets and Puritans.* London, 1915.

Green, John Richard. *History of the People of England.* New York, n. d.

Haller, William, ed. *Tracts on Liberty in the Puritan Revolution, 1638-1647.* Edited with a commentary. 3 vols., New York, 1934.

Halley, Robert. *Lancashire, its Puritanism and Nonconformity.* 2 vols., London, 1869.

Hibbert-Ware, Samuel. *Lancashire Memorials of the Rebellion, MDCCXV.* . . . 2 vols. in one, Chetham Society, 1845.

James, Margaret. *Social Problems and Policy during the Protestant Revolution, 1640-1660.* London, 1930.

Jones, W. H. R. *Salisbury* [Diocesan Histories]. London, 1880.

Jordan, Wilbur K. *The Development of Religious Toleration in England.* 4 vols., London and Cambridge, 1932-1940.

Ladell, A. R. *Richard Baxter, Puritan and Mystic.* London, 1925.

Lathbury, Thomas. *A History of the Non-jurors, their Controversies and Writings.* London, 1845.

Legg, J. Wickham. *English Church Life from the Restoration to the Tractarian Movement.* London, 1914.

Lyon, Thomas, *The Theory of Religious Liberty in England, 1603-1639.* Cambridge, 1937.

Mackintosh, Sir James. *History of the Revolution in England in 1688.* London, 1834.

McLachlan, H. *English Education under the Test Acts: The History of the Nonconformist Academies, 1662-1820.* Manchester, 1931.

Masson, David. *Life of John Milton narrated in Connexion with the Political, Ecclesiastical, and Literary History of his Time.* 7 vols., London and New York, 1877-1896.

Overton, John Henry. *Life in the English Church, 1660-1714.* London, 1885.

Pattison, Mark. "Tendencies of Religious Thought in England, 1688-1750," *Essays and Reviews.* London, 1860.

Powicke, F. J. *Life of the Reverend Richard Baxter.* London, 1924.

The Protestant Dissenters Magazine, 6 vols., 1794-1799.

Robertson, H. M. *Aspects of the Rise of Economic Individualism.* Cambridge, 1933.

Shaw, William A. *A History of the English Church during the Civil Wars and the Commonwealth.* London, 1916.

Skeats, H. S., and Miall, C. S. *History of the Free Churches of England.* London, 1844.

Stoughton, J. *History of Religion from the Opening of the Long Parliament to the End of the Eighteenth Century.* New and revised edition, London, 1887.

Sykes, Norman. *Church and State in England in the Eighteenth Century.* Cambridge, 1934.

———. *Edmund Gibson, Bishop of London, 1669-1748: A Study in Politics and Religion in the Eighteenth Century.* Oxford, 1926.

Victoria County History of London. 3 vols., Westminster, 1909.

Whiting, Charles E. *Studies in English Puritanism from the Restoration to the Revolution, 1660-1688.* New York, 1931.

Wren, M. London in the Puritan Revolution. Unpublished Doctoral Dissertation, University of Iowa, 1939.

INDEX

Acts on religion, Corporation Act, 24; Act of Uniformity, 24, 30 n; Conventicle Act, 24, 35, 37; Five Mile Act, 24, 33; Clarendon Code, 24; protest of London ministers, 25; early reasons for, 25; failure of, 26; economic effects, 29; Oxford Parliament, 33; nullified by great fire, 33, 34; first Press Act, 37; Test Act 1673, 37, 47; Sunday Observance Act, 56; Toleration Act, 74; repeal of Clarendon Code in part, 76, 79; aid growth of dissent, 85; Bill of Rights, 71; Occasional Conformity Act, 93; Schism Act, 93

Anglicans, in office under Commonwealth, 13; impatience under Charles I, 17; conference at Savoy, 20; bitterness toward Nonconformity, 20, 21; pamphlets on Savoy, 22; effects of Savoy, 22; effects of Clarendon Code on church and clergy, 26, 28, 29, 32, 34; help government to enforce Code, 26; complaint of growing Nonconformity, 37; weakened in Parliament, 44; assert absolute power of King, 45; charged with favoring Catholics, 50; laity support Nonconformists, 53; emphasize religious life, 61; after 1688, 81; effects of toleration on, 87; mentioned, 62, 63, 67, 78, 79

Anne, Queen, favored High Church party, 87; Convocation's report to, 88; dismissed Convocation, 93; death, 93; mentioned, 87, 92

Army, radicalism in, 12; Rump gave rise to military dictatorship, 12

Articles of visitation, 28

Atterbury, Francis, leads opposition to Nonconformity, 92; forced abroad, 93

Baillie, Robert, Scottish commissioner, 11

Baptist, few in 1604, 7, 14; accept second indulgence, 41, 42; refuse occasional conformity, 91; mentioned, 48, 56

Baxter, Richard, farewell sermon, 25 n.; confers with Low Churchmen, 48; arrested in London, 48; active in later period, 54, 55; upholds comprehension, 55, 58; in prison, 61, 63; restates Presbyterian position, 85; mentioned, 21, 36, 64, 79

Bill of Rights, see Acts on religion

Bristol, diocese of, 51

Buckingham, Duke of, see Villiers, George

Bunyan, John, in prison, 60, 62

Burnet, Gilbert, flees to Continent, 60, 65; made Bishop of Salisbury, 74; twits Compton on education, 87; mentioned, 50

Calamy, Edmund, 21, 25 n., 36

Calamy, Edmund (younger), 62